M000206499

THE OBSTACLE COURSE

THE LONG ROAD TO DISCIPLESHIP

Dan —
Your advise in the early 90's saved our program — I want to thank you and Shirley for opening your home to our city kids and for supporting our graduates missionaries and orphanage in East Africa

Bill (Coach)

Published by Mindstir Media, LLC
45 Lafayette Rd | Suite 181| North Hampton, NH 03862 | USA
1.800.767.0531 | www.mindstirmedia.com

Printed in the United States of America
ISBN-13: 978-1-7329482-5-9
Library of Congress Control Number: 2018963178

THE OBSTACLE COURSE

THE LONG ROAD TO DISCIPLESHIP

Bill Spanjer III

MINDSTIR MEDIA

DEDICATION

I would like to dedicate this book to:
My Lord and Savior, Jesus Christ, who by His sacrifice gave
me eternal life.

My mother and father, who taught me right from wrong.

My wonderful wife, who typed this book and put up with the
wild ride I took her on.

To my daughter, Kristy, whom God sent as an angel from
heaven to save my life.

And

A final thank you and farewell to:
Piper PA90 Super Cubs and "Champs"
John Deere Tractors
Brown Swiss Cows
Ford Trucks
R-2800 Engines

And

Old Dogs, Children, and
Lake Country Red Wine

Solo Christo Gloria

ACKNOWLEDGMENTS

To those who helped me, encouraged me, taught me and to those who prayed for me, and sacrificed with me on my long life's journey to find and serve my Lord and Savior; thank you from the deepest recesses of my heart.

Jesus Christ, my Lord
My father and my mother
My wife, Kathleen and our children,
Bill IV, Dan, Tim, Stephen, and Kristy
Bob Hoppe
Maj. Gen. Ralph Spanjer
Rear Adm. Lawrence Daspit
Professor Jim "Buck" Hatch
Dr. George Cannon, Ph.D.
Pop Suplee
Rev. Carl Luthman
Don Castner
Dr. R. C. Sproul
Dr. Douglas Culver
Ron Bonagura
Roger Christine
Art Luse
Ken Schliphak
Al Teplitz
Johnny Pollack
Erik Vellenga
Rich Kuperus

Eric McCaffrey

Debra Bailey

Ed Schrader

Vinnie Farina

Mike DeVries

Henry, Buddy, Rich, and Hank DeVries

Rev. Dr. John Vance

Rev. Dr. Kevin Chiarot

Rev. Ezra Williams

Stephanie Snyder

Mike Bonagura

Phil Shafer

Eric Parks

David Stein

Cindy Leventis

Chris Schweiger

Maria Flores

Judy Goldberg

John Liu

Dr. Nathan Gill

Stacy Kuperus

Andrew Spanjer

My Staff:
Allen Bailey
Scarlet Devens
Cheryl Goodrich
Amy Kumicinski
Joseph and Ashley Maina
Jenna Montanye
Cindy Schoch

And all the others who have been with me in my life
and co-workers together with Christ, to help make the ministry
for our Lord successful, thank you.

TABLE OF CONTENTS

INTRODUCTION 13

PROLOGUE THE RAINY NIGHT 15

CHAPTER I THE WAR YEARS, 1935–1949....................................19

CHAPTER II THE PRANKSTERS 30

CHAPTER III PARRIS ISLAND AND THE OBSTACLE COURSE 39

CHAPTER IV BOB HOPPE AND THE USS BOSTON..............................47

CHAPTER V TROUBLE ON LAND AND SEA 54

CHAPTER VI MONKEY ON MY BACK...70

CHAPTER VII EVERY WIND OF DOCTRINE 84

CHAPTER VIII THE AVIATION DEVIATION, PART I: THE "CHAMP"............98

CHAPTER IX AVIATION DEVIATION, PART II: THE SILVER DOLLAR 109

CHAPTER X AVIATION DEVIATION, PART III: NEVER A DULL MOMENT ..119

CHAPTER XI SPAN EAST AIRLINES AND WEDDING BELLS 128

CHAPTER XII CRISIS IN FARM COUNTRY 139

CHAPTER XIII CAPTURED 151

CHAPTER XIV FOLLOW ME—TO THE INNER CITY...............................165

CHAPTER XV VALUE OF THE GOAL 176

CHAPTER XVI THE BLENDED CHURCH 184

CHAPTER XVII MIRACLES ON FLEURY ROAD 195

CHAPTER XVIII CHAPEL FIELD...205

CHAPTER XIX NO MONEY, NO PROBLEM......................................216

CHAPTER XX BEYOND THE CLASSROOM.......................................233

EPILOGUE 245

OBSERVATIONS..245

ABOUT THE FAMILY 255

SOURCES AND REFERENCES 257

INTRODUCTION

In this book, you will read about a boy growing up in two separate homes during the war years. I had two loving parents with entirely two different personalities. I think my high school experience will be a little bit bizarre but somewhat typical for many kids. My life on the farm will be the envy of most boys and my hitch in the Marine Corps, although it started somewhat tragically, ended on a high note. The principles my father, in particular, taught me will be explained in detail, and if followed, will make anyone successful in life, whatever profession or job they pursue. These have stayed with me all my days. They account heavily for whatever accomplishments I may have had. I believe the Lord gave them to me through my dad.

My aviation deviation will be somewhat scary, but the things I learned there gave me the knowledge and courage to do ministry. I hope the reader will pay close attention to Chapters 13 through 20. I believe the story told there is the key to opening God's resources to the crucified Christian. I believe these chapters prove God's faithfulness to those willing to sacrifice all to work in His vineyard.

I have intentionally tried not to make this book a family album. You will not read much about them in the text. However, God has blessed my wife and me with five children. They are all serving the Lord in different areas. I have included a blurb on them in the back of the book ("About the Family").

I am quite opinionated in the conclusions I have reached in my college years (particularly my exit from Catholicism and my critique of Protestant denominationalism) and later my view of the contemporary Christian church. They may offend some, but

I trust I have leaned on Scripture enough to support them.

As I will say in several chapters, I am not an intellectual or scholar. I am just a simple country boy layman, leaning heavily on Martin Luther's principle of Biblical perspicuity and trying to make sense out of the Biblical mandates for Christians as related to our present Christian culture. These are my experiences and conclusions. But I am convinced they are Biblical. Anyway, I hope the principles, experiences, and adventures, particularly in the early chapters, will cause the reader to appreciate the values herein conveyed. In the later chapters, I hope you will see the Biblical mandates for discipleship and God's faithfulness to His servants in ministry, and the difficulties presented to these men and women by the contemporary Christian church.

Beyond simply relating my experiences springing from the obstacle course, my true desire for this book is to encourage the reader to see that the gospel of grace is received by faith, to understand the importance of Reformation orthodoxy, to know the path of true discipleship and to challenge his or her church toward missions. I hope when we disagree, we will all let Scripture be our guide. Until Jesus leads us down the Emmaus Road, this is my story, and I'm stickin' to it.

– Bill Spanjer III

PROLOGUE

THE RAINY NIGHT

I recall an incident that still makes me shiver when I think about it today. I had just gotten my flight instructor rating and wanted to fly day and night, regardless of the weather. Al Botwin was one of my students. He passed his written exam for his private license and his flight test. Now he wanted to be checked out for night flying, and I set him up for the next Tuesday. It was a rainy night, but the sky was crystal clear with a ceiling of about 6,500 feet. Despite the rain, it was a calm night for flying. Al and I did four or five landings; he was good, so I signed him off for night flying. We said good night, and I went to the airport office to fill out my paperwork for the day. It was about nine thirty p.m. I sat at a desk near the big plate glass windows in the office listening to the rain, which was running down the windows. All of a sudden a face appeared outside, directly in front of me. Dripping wet, it was pressed to the window—I thought he was crying. We stared at each other for a second; in an instant, we both turned our heads toward the door, and a dash began on both sides of the window—he to get in, and me to lock him out. Unfortunately, he had a clear path, and I had a counter in my way, and I lost.

A short, husky man, distraught and crying, entered accompanied by another man. The story, as these two shared it, was that the crying man's mother was on her deathbed in Wilkes Barre, Pennsylvania, and he needed to get to see her right away. The tall gentleman with him said that he had driven him to the airport, and had money enough to give him to pay for the flight in advance. I looked at the "distance chart" hanging on my wall. Wilkes Barre—Scranton Airport was about 175 miles to the west, about an hour and a half's flight at $100 an hour. That would come to about $300, as the charge would be round trip, so $325 to cover ground time, and he plunked down $500 bill and told me to keep the change.

I was excited. This night flight would give me over thirteen hours in the cockpit that day. I wanted to fly day and night, so this fit my plans perfectly. I decided that I ought to find a co-pilot, but who could I get at that hour? It was ten p.m., and everyone I could think of would be ready for bed. Well, I thought, it will be a quick flight, and I'll be home before one a.m. So I went looking for a plane with enough gas to get me to Wilkes Barre and back. I could do this on my own. Big mistake. I should have found someone—anyone—to go with me.

I knew that flying at night in a single engine was risky, but my Twin Aztec was on a charter that night, and the only plane I could find with full tanks was 454MD, Dr. Rothschild's Cherokee 180.

I strapped my husky passenger into the seat behind me—a move I later discovered may have saved my life. Most passengers like to sit in the co-pilot's seat to see what is going on. As we made our ascent out of the airport and we flew over the Hudson Valley, the night was so clear that the raindrops on my left window sparkled with the distant New York City lights. I climbed to about 5,500 feet and leveled off. As the lights of Middletown and then Port Jervis faded behind us, we were surrounded by the eerie darkness of the Pennsylvania hills.

There was no horizon, and there were no checkpoints. I was flying by instrument and radio navigation alone. About an hour into the flight, my passenger began crying again, and I tried, from my seat, to calm him down. Suddenly, he started shouting,

"I want to die! I want to die" and began wrestling against the seat belt in an attempt to unfasten it. It seemed clear to me that what he wanted was to get at the co-pilot's controls. If he got to those controls, he could have ripped them out, and we would have been a burned spot somewhere in the forest of Eastern Pennsylvania. Trying to keep my focus, I was flying the plane with one hand and trying to fight him off with the other as he kept struggling and screaming, "I want to die!" I prayed, "God, please let the seat belt hold," when all of a sudden there, through the darkness, I saw the glow of the lights of Wilkes Barre on the horizon. And with relief, I spotted the green rotating beacon of the airport. Meanwhile, my arm was getting weak trying to keep my screaming passenger in his seat. I pointed the nose of the Cherokee at the green light and started a power-on descent. As soon as the runway lights became clear and I started hollering, "We are landing, calm down! Calm down!" And finally, he began to settle down.

I powered onto the runway and hit the brakes hard. Safe on the ground, I felt my muscles relax. I could handle anything now… I thought. As we taxied up to the terminal, I saw a group of men standing outside. As we reached the building, I saw a group of men on the flight ramp. They walked over to the plane. "Who are these guys?" I thought as I parked, shut off the engine, and opened the door.

One gentleman came over and asked, "Are you Mr. Spanjer?" I thought, how did he know my name? When I told him who I was, and asked who he was, he flashed a badge and answered, "I am Special Agent (so and so) from the F.B.I. You have just transported an escaped felon across state lines. Your passenger escaped from a suicide watch at Rockland State Psychiatric Hospital."

"Oh, good grief," I groaned in my mind. "I almost died in a

plane crash, and now I am in trouble with the F.B.I." But before I could fully contemplate what that might mean, one of the agents took my passenger into custody and turned to me and said, "You can go; we'll be in touch." Wasting no time, I cranked 454MD up and headed out onto the taxiway. My heart was still pounding, so I pulled the plane around and sat at the end of the runway for a long time, trying to settle myself down. Why had this mental patient's seat belt not come open? Airplane seatbelts at that time took merely a flick to open, so why did this man, with all of his trying, fail to open his? I gave God my sincere thanks that He had controlled that from happening. When I finally got the Cherokee in the air, I flew home, tied it down, and went to bed. The next morning I drove to the airport but never said anything about the previous night. To my relief, the F.B.I. never contacted me, but I thought to myself, how did I get into this mess anyway?

Bill with 454MD

CHAPTER I

THE WAR YEARS
1935–1949

For thou didst form my inward parts: Thou didst cover me in my mother's womb. I will give thanks unto thee; for I am fearfully and wonderfully made: Wonderful are thy works; And that my soul knoweth right well. My frame was not hidden from thee, When I was made in secret, And curiously wrought in the lowest parts of the earth. Thine eyes did see mine unformed substance; And in thy book they were all written, Even the days that were ordained for me, When as yet there was none of them (Psalm 139:13-16, ASV).

It all began on April 30, 1935. I was born to Eleanor and William Spanjer, Jr. My mother taught me to believe in God, Christ, and the Holy Spirit. I never remember a day in my life that I did not believe. My father taught me by his words and actions how to live a life of character, a Christian life. The only problem was that my parents divorced when I was two years old. They were totally mismatched; my mother liked the social life, cocktail parties, bridge, and dancing. My father, the outdoors, horses, skiing, and farming. Once when I had a farm of my own, I tried to get my mother to come to the farm; she said, "I can't come, there are no sidewalks there." That said it all. What does a true city gal have in common with a manure-spattered country boy? Nothing. It's like stirring oil into water. So, I began a life of weekdays home with Mom and weekends with dad. Thank God, the breakup was compatible; they were truly concerned about each other. I can remember when my dad would bring me home on Sunday nights, they would talk for hours at a time. As I remember, my dad bought my mother a car to replace a worn-out one. I saw they really cared for one another and they lived up to their character. That never left me.

One Friday night, my father picked me up and said, "This weekend we are going to look at farms in Sussex County, New Jersey. I want to buy one." Well, we spent Saturday looking at farms. Sunday, he wanted to look at one more in Branchville, NJ. That Sunday happened to be December 7, 1941. As we drove through the rolling hills of Sussex County in my dad's '39 Ford woody station wagon, the radio would cut out in the valleys and became clear again on the hilltops. On one hill we pulled over and heard the news—the Japanese had bombed Pearl Harbor. This event changed my life and thousands of others forever.

My mother was a schoolteacher, who taught fourth grade at Paramus Elementary School. My father was a businessman who was president of Spanjer Brothers, a wood-sign letter and display company with a factory in Newark, New Jersey. Now that factory would change to provide items and materials for the war effort.

When we got done looking at farms that Sunday, my dad asked me which one I liked. I said, "The one in Branchville, Dad."

He said, "I do too." The farm was nestled in a valley with a 300-foot hill on the west side right behind the barns and house. To the east were open rolling fields. The farm had a stream running through it. The property was beautiful. The buildings, on the other hand, were dilapidated—barns falling down, silos leaning, the fields rocky, twenty cows but only half milking.

What a mess. The house, although rustic, had no running water, no central heat, no electric, and no indoor plumbing. There was a two-hole outhouse about seventy feet from the front door. I can remember many winter nights holding my hands on the seat to melt the frost and partially warm the seat before sitting down. On weekdays I had all the comforts the 1940s could offer—heat, water from faucets, and a bathroom. My father later turned the farm—we called it Valley Farm—into a showcase farm. The agricultural departments of several universities visited to see how it was done.

Valley Farm, 1949
Taken from high hill behind the farm

Well, in 1945, the war with Germany was over. The rationing of gasoline was over; off went the black paint I had to put on half my mother's headlights on her 1940 Willys coup, which she called "Badilia," to prevent Nazi bombers from seeing us at night. But most of all, soon to be gone but never forgotten, were the black frames around the stars hanging on thousands of doors throughout our town and our country for the fallen who did not come home. The sight of these stars with black frames haunted me throughout my childhood.

Late in 1945, my mother met Air Force Major Jim Dennett, at a social club. He had just returned from combat in Europe. They fell in love and married, and Mom and I were on our way to Germany as dependents. Jim was assigned to the European Occupation Forces under General Dwight D. Eisenhower. Meanwhile, my father found a carpenter, Eddie Longcore, to help him restore our farm. Eddie's wife had a sister, Olga, whose husband had been killed while serving with General Patton's Third Army in the Battle of the Bulge in France. She had a son, Rodger, who had never known his father. They dated and were married that year. Now I had two families.

My father had seven sisters and two brothers. His father, William Spanjer Sr. and his brother, Henry Spanjer, emigrated from Holland. They were true rugged individualists and Olympic-class boxers and gymnasts; Henry won a gold medal for boxing in the 1904 Olympics. They eventually started a wooden sign, letter, and display business (Spanjer Brothers) in Newark, New Jersey, and Chicago, Illinois, respectively. I inherited this spirit of rugged individualism and later became fiercely independent. God had to tame me, but I always had a strong belief in what I could do on my own with God's inspiration and help. This spirit benefited me well in fulfilling my later calling, and I feel God greatly honored it. But being one who would take big risks and wade into waters where others feared to tread, left me with no close friends in later life. I have had many good friends that helped me along the way, and I greatly cherished them. I have no close friends. There is a song in the Southern Gospel circles that says "when in old age, old friends, what a prize, treasure, and comfort." If I could do it over, I would try to balance better my social life and drive for ministry.

The heart is deceitful above all things and desperately wicked: who can know it? (Jeremiah 17:9, KJV)

The verse I chose for the rest of this chapter has provided much controversy in our culture, theological schools, the church, and among Christians. The argument goes like this: on the one hand, the naturalists and liberal theologians say man by nature is basically good and that his bad behavior is learned from his influences or his desires for wealth, prestige, and power. On the other hand, Christians and conservative theologians teach that man (human beings) is by nature depraved, that this happens at birth. Good behavior by man is brought about by three factors. First, is by teaching (learning) what is good and right based on an objective standard (God's laws). Second, man is restrained by peer-pressure by social acceptability and civil law to do right, which is reinforced by the government (police, military, etc.), and third, by regenerating the human depraved condition by the power of God's Spirit (being born again or born anew) reversing our depraved nature (John 3:3, II Corinthians 5:17).

Thousands upon thousands of men have died defending us against the intrinsic evil heart of mankind. I wondered, when are we going to learn this critical Biblical truth? I did in the story that follows.

Mom and I boarded the *Saint Rosemarie*, bound for Germany in the winter of 1946. We arrived in the port of Bremerhaven near Hamburg. We stayed three months in Ansbach in South East Germany while Jim awaited final assignment to the airfield at Oberpfaffenhofen, Southern Bavaria. Upon that transfer, a very nice home was provided for us in the town of Gauteng about eight miles from the air base. It was a beautiful town nestled in a valley at the north end of the Starnberg Sea, a great lake near the Bavarian Alps. It was close to Hitler's Eagle's nest and King Ludwig's castle at Neuschwanstein. As a child, I was so impressed with the Bavarian Alps and with Neuschwanstein that King Ludwig built in 1884. It was the most beautiful structure I had ever seen. Built on a mountain peak in the Alps near Forggensee Lake, it was over two hundred feet tall, now a classic castle that every child dreams about. Many Germans say Ludwig was insane, I say he was a genius.

Neuschwannstein Castle, Bavaria, Germany

Oberpfaffenhofen was a maintenance facility that serviced

the airplanes that flew the Berlin Airlift. Planes would be routed out of the Airlift and go to Oberpfaffenhofen for maintenance and repair. A bus (converted 6x6 truck) ran from Gauteng three times a day; eight a.m., noon, and eight p.m. for military wives and children wanting to go to the air base for shopping at the PX (post exchange) and the movies. On Saturdays, I would tell my mom that I was going to the base to see a movie. In reality, I would go to the flight operations building at the air base and sit at the door begging pilots as they came out with their flight orders to take me along with them. They would fly a recondi- tioned C-47 (known as the Goonie Bird) famous in WW II, or a C-54 four-engine cargo plane to Wiesbaden Germany where it would be routed back into the Berlin Airlift. It was strictly pro- hibited for dependents to fly on these trips, but I was just a kid wanting to fly. "Come on kid, you can go with us, but don't tell your father." I would often sit in a jump seat right behind the pilots. On one such trip, the pilot said, "Take my seat kid" and I got behind the flight controls. He took the time to explain the instruments, the turn and bank indicator, the rpm gauges, the airspeed indicator. Then he let me turn to different headings on the compass. WOW! I was hooked. I knew right there I wanted to be a pilot.

Usually, there would be a two- to three-hour turnaround before the pilots would get assigned a plane to take back to Oberpfaffenhofen. Sometimes I would play with some German kids in the rubble of Wiesbaden. Other times the pilots would take me to lunch. On one such occasion, they wanted to stop off at a masseuse. So, we all piled into a jeep and drove to a hotel only partially bombed out. There they left me in the hands of a very large German lady who stripped me down, wrapped me in hot towels, plunged me into a mineral bath then proceeded to beat me to a pulp with her very large hands. The experience was somewhat frightening for a kid of twelve, but I felt good as we got into the jeep for our return to the airfield.

We landed about seven thirty, just in time for me to get the last bus to Gauting. As we drove by the movie theater, I glanced at the marquee to make sure I got the movie title right when I got quizzed by my mom on what happened that day.

It was true that you could buy a suit of clothes for a pack of cigarette, and shoes for two smokes. One of my German friends' families gave me a motorbike for two number-ten cans of peaches, which I requisitioned from my mother's pantry. They couldn't use the bike because no gas was available in Germany at that time. I siphoned some gas from my stepfather's jeep. Often, I would ride until dark around the beautiful German countryside.

I went to a one-room schoolhouse in the village of Unterbrunn about three miles from the air bases. We had about eighteen students from first grade to twelfth. We were taught in groups.

Bill raising flag over schoolhouse in Unterbrunn, Germany

General Eisenhower issued an order in 1946 that all U.S. servicemen and their dependents must visit one of the concentration camps while in Germany. One day it was our turn to go. Eighteen children, two teachers, and a couple of parents climbed into a 6x6 bus and went to Dachau. As we went through the town and approached the concentration camp the smell of burning flesh was in the air. My teachers and parents held handkerchiefs over their mouths and noses. As we went through the oven chambers, the small became worse; mind you, this was a year and a half after the camp was liberated. The stench was overwhelming. To this day, I can still smell it in my memory. Anyone who says the Germans in that town didn't know what was going on, they are liars. The smell permeated everything, the homes, the shops, the businesses.

We saw the large metal stretchers on wheels with long handles to wheel some live victims into the ovens. The ovens were designed with doors that would allow the handles to stick out so that workers could retrieve the ashes without getting burned. We saw rows of hanging trees where victims hung. We saw endless plots where victims were buried alive and then machine-gunned into shallow graves. We walked through the so-called showers which were really gas chambers where thousands were gassed. I remember the big hole in the wall, blasted, so it could never be used again. The gas chamber was located next to the long row of ovens. Our staff sergeant guide explained that this was so victims, some dead or semi-conscious could be easily taken to the ovens. It looked like an assembly line to me. Not only Hitler and his staff but regular people—husbands, mothers, children, churchgoers—willingly took part in this horrendous cruelty. Had they no compassion, had they no conscience? Was this learned behavior or did it spring from a depraved nature that could act with no consequence? "The heart of man is desperately wicked." Even as a twelve-year-old I thanked God that in the end, He would provide a consequence. One sign read, "It was true. Let's see that this never happens again."

Sign at Dachau extermination camp, 1947

That afternoon we went to the Nuremberg trials. There were about twenty on trial. I recognized two of the defendants that my teacher had described earlier—Herman Goering and Albert Speer. Goering was the head of Hitler's Luftwaffe, a big heavy-set man with a fat face. Albert Speer's looks were distinct, sharp features as I remember. He was the architect of Hitler's Third Reich. Goering was sentenced to death by hanging but took a cyanide pill in his cell and died. Speer pleaded that he did not know of Hitler's atrocities and received a prison sentence. I always believed he was complicit in Hitler's atrocities. Did he not have a nose? Could he not smell? Also, that afternoon Ilse Koch was on trial. As they bought in the artifacts, lamp shades, pocketbooks with tattooed pictures taken from dying and dead victims. My teachers tried to shield them from our view, but I saw them. I was only a few feet from the table where they were placed. Ilse was convicted but avoided the hangman's noose by becoming pregnant by a prison guard. Both Albert and Ilse were later released. I am eighty-two years old; the atrocities committed in Dachau and the visions and smells of that day have haunted me every day of my life.

In 1949, Jim Dennett was reassigned to the U.S. Mom and I and hundreds of other U.S. dependents boarded a converted troop ship for our return to the States. As we approached the New York Harbor, the ship listed to port as everyone stood at the rails to see the Statue of Liberty. Now without a doubt, all of us knew what the monument stood for. With visions of what we had touched, seen, and smelled, we knew exactly what over 250,000 men gave their life for. We were glad to be back in The Land of Liberty!

CHAPTER II

THE PRANKSTERS

When I was a child, I spake as a child, I understood as a child, I thought as a child: but when I became a man, I put away childish things (I Corinthians 13:11, KJV).

In 1949 America was a happy place. Peace reigned, prosperity grew. Jim was transferred to Salina, Kansas where he was immediately discharged. It seemed that he had become an alcoholic. That was attributed to his last assignment at Oberpfaffenhofen where he was made Officer in Charge of the Officer's Club. For him, the booze flowed all day and all evening long. He succumbed to it. It was not long after that that my mother let me go back to live with my father. I was fifteen years old, back on the farm and starting my high school years. What more could a boy of fifteen ask for: John Deere tractors, Brown Swiss cows, a Willys jeep, Ford cars and trucks, friends, girlfriends, and sports.

As far as sports were concerned, I loved Joe Lewis. I remember once my father and my uncle Ralph (who was the New York State Golden Gloves champion in the late 1930s) took me to see Joe fight. Everybody was mad when Joe knocked his opponent out in the third round. Well, it was a "bum a month"; what did we expect? Doc Blanchard and Glenn Davis were my heroes in football. But my real sport was baseball. I loved the Brooklyn Dodgers. The "Bums," Jackie Robinson, Roy Campanella, and Peewee Reese made baseball come alive for me. I learned that if the Dodgers were losing by five in the eighth inning, don't turn the radio off because they'd pull it out in the bottom of the ninth. The Dodger Symphony that played behind home plate went crazy. At the time they were the thrill of my life.

As far as music was concerned, I loved the Grand Ole Opry. I'd go to sleep every night with a transistor radio at my pillow. Jim Reeves was my favorite: "Four Walls," "Welcome to My World," "He'll Have to Go." In my estimation, he was the best male voice ever. And George Jones with "Grand Tour," Hank Williams, and Johnny Cash, were also great. As far as women were concerned, Patsy Cline was the best. Her "Tennessee Waltz" ended all our dances and proms. Tammy Wynette, Brenda Lee and Emmylou Harris's "Making Believe" topped the women for me.

I never was a big movie buff, but I couldn't resist anything with Randolph Scott, John Wayne, Gary Cooper, Rhonda Fleming, or Jane Wyman in it.

I had four serious girlfriends before meeting my future wife, Kathleen Bartels in 1967. Martha McLean was my high school sweetheart. They called it "puppy love," but she meant more to me than that. There was Cathy Kroll from Hamburg, New Jersey. I invited her to my high school prom. On a walk before the prom on her dock, I picked her up in my arms. She dared me to throw her in the lake, so I did. Her dress came floating to the top. I had to jump in to spread the humiliation around. A side note: she wrote me regularly while I was in Parris Island boot camp. However, we received our mail daily but were not allowed to read it until Sundays. She smothered them in perfume, so I was the butt of many jokes. One weekday I couldn't resist so I sneaked a peek at her letter. The D.I. caught me. While standing at attention, his one blow to my face knocked me out. When I came to he made me eat the letter. I never got a chance to read it.

There was Julie Galup, a beautiful petite blonde. She was a championship horse-jumping rider. We dated until I went away to college. And then there was Betty Russell, a true Southern belle with all the Southern charm. She cast a spell on me. I will talk about that all-consuming attraction in a later chapter.

Reflecting on my childhood, I learned important lessons from my mother. In addition to etiquette and the proper use of the English language, she taught me to love and honor God, to be a gentleman, to be respectful to adults, especially women, to protect the opposite sex and to be a moral and ethical person.

My mother was Roman Catholic, and we attended mass regularly. In the order of the mass, the people would sometimes stand, often sit, and occasionally kneel. I noticed that when we were called to kneel, most people would "kneel-sit." I thought that was most disrespectful to God, and I determined to kneel no matter how painful to my knees. I loved God and knew He had something special for me to do later in life.

My father was very strict. He believed in the belt as the ultimate punishment which I received a number of times. Many afternoons I would sit at a desk memorizing my times tables while my friends played outside. But I learned from Dad to obey him and all authority, to work hard every day whether I liked the job or not, to say 'yes sir' and 'no sir' to my elders and to love my country and to honor those who gave their lives for it. In addition, I was to give my all to those who paid me, to be honest to a fault and to protect all females. These were not suggestions; they were demanded of me. I always felt safe, secure, and protected by both of my parents, particularly by my mother, but as a young boy, my father was my idol.

My high school years, particularly eleventh and twelfth grades were prank years, but generally, I was not interested in them. Putting toilet paper in someone's car was stupid to me. However, there were a few pranks that I got lassoed into. I didn't want to include them here, but my wife insisted. So here goes.

The first thing you have to know about Sussex High School is that it was located in a large agricultural community. Dairy farming was the major industry followed by produce (there were many thousands of acres of flat black dirt in the northeast part of our country). Following those were apple orchards and chicken farms. Because of this, our school provided a vocational agricultural program. These kids were called Aggies in our school. In the cafeteria, the far table in the corner was the Aggie table because we would all meet there for lunch. Now nothing good ever came from this table. In fact, many an ingenious plot was hatched there that when enacted, even the F.B.I. if called in, could not solve.

A close friend of mine in the Aggies was Louie Hardick. Now Louie was a little rough around the edges. He lived with his mom in a cottage near our farm. They were poor, but Louie always came to school neat and clean. One day at the Aggie lunch table Bill Ricky said to Louie, "I'll bet you $10 you wouldn't kiss Mrs. Jones in class." Now one thing Louie could not resist was a dare. Ricky added, "I'll give Spanjer the $10 to hold." Now Jones was our literature teacher. She was middle-aged, attractive, petite and dressed meticulously. She had natural auburn red hair, no hairs out of place. She loved literature and particularly poetry. However, Longfellow and Shakespeare were not the first choices on an Aggie's reading list. The extent of our reading was Yogi Berra's quotes and Bob Hope's jokes. There were six Aggies in that class, and we all suffered through it every day.

Well, the next day Mrs. Jones stood in front of her desk reading, I think Byron, and we were supposed to take notes. I was sitting near the back in the center row. Louie was seated midway in the row to my right. I saw him intentionally break his pencil point on his desk, then hold it up to Mrs. Jones and signal toward the pencil sharpener behind her. She nodded, and Louie went up to sharpen his pencil. I thought, wow, this scheme is about to go down! We all thought Louie would walk by her and give her a peck on the cheek. But Louie grabbed Mrs. Jones, bent her backward over his knee, embraced her, and planted a big one right on her lips! Well, the class went bonkers. Louie straightened her up. She was shaken, had to steady herself on her desk. Her face turned as red as her hair. Louie was sent to the principal's office, and Mrs. Jones took the rest of the week off.

The next morning the six of us Aggies were called into the principal's office. Mr. Wagonhurst had six chairs lined up in front of his desk. Normally a laidback gentleman, he was irate. He started out, "I know Louie would not do this if someone didn't put him up to it. Who was it?" He started with Ricky. "Did you have anything to do with this?"

Ricky said, "I don't know what's got into Louie."

"Spanjer, what do you know?"

I said, "I don't know, Mr. Wagonhurst. Louie is very unpredictable." Meanwhile, I still had the $10 in my pocket that Ricky gave me.

So it went down the line. McDonough was on the end. We all held our breath. McDonough had a reputation for telling it like it was. What would he say? Would he give us away? McDonough said, "I think Louie had the hots for Mrs. Jones."

Well, Mr. Wagonhurst exploded. "If I find out any of you had anything to do with this I'll suspend all of you." Well, we all clammed up until it all blew over.

That little prank backfired, but we didn't learn. That winter the school hired an assistant ag teacher, Mr. Howard. Now Howie, as we called him (though not to his face) was a wise guy. No one in school liked him. He had a perpetual smirk on his face. He would intentionally ask difficult questions in class, and when you couldn't answer correctly, he would publicly mock you.

Now, Mr. Howard drove a foreign sports car, with a puny little engine in it. However, Howie thought he was an Indianapolis 500 driver. Our school's parking lot was gravel. Howie would come into it every morning, wheels spinning in the gravel, do a k-turn, and back up, again wheels spinning, to his parking space right behind a large telephone pole. After school he would do the same thing, spinning his wheels out of the parking lot to show off. On a road or dry surface if he popped the clutch that puny engine would have died. The joke among us Aggies was his car couldn't pull a wet turd out of a grease bucket. Once, an Aggie brought a little quarter-horsepower sowing machine motor to school and put it on his desk with a note, reading, "If you want more horsepower, change your engine with this." Well, smirky Howard doubled down on us after that with his snide comments and spinning tires in the gravel parking lot.

One day at the Aggie lunch table, someone suggested that we take a chain and tie it to Howie's bumper and put it around the telephone pole he so proudly backed up to each morning. Wow! We all thought that would be a great "get-back" prank. Well, no one had a chain. I said, "I have one, a twenty-footer we used once in a while to pull logs out of the woods. I'll bring it in." I could hardly carry my athletic bag to school the next day with the chain in it. The senior-class Aggies took it and second period did their dastardly deed. At three o'clock we had our faces plastered to the windows in the science room. Four senior girls were standing around in the parking lot. We knew Howie would really show off for a crowd, especially for girls. Well, Howie came out, got in his little pea-popper, as we called it, pumped the gas, and with a smirky smile and a wave to the girls, threw into first gear, popped the clutch, spun the tires, and was off. Bang! The girls dispersed. I looked, the bumper was still there. I turned to McDonough, "What happened?" The seniors told me they couldn't hook the chain to the bumper, so they hooked it to the axel. The chain broke and ripped the axel and left wheel from the frame! We hightailed it to baseball practice just in time to get in for attendance. Our alibi was clinched! We were at baseball practice. At that time we saw a police car drive into the campus. I heard later that the cop who investigated the incident was a former Aggie and that he chuckled at seeing Howie's car. However, he took the chain as evidence.

Well, Howie got his car fixed and became very subdued toward us. He drove into and out of the parking lot very carefully. About a month later, Howie found another job and resigned. Someone in class led us in a little ditty, "We're sad to see you go, we're sad to see you go. We hope to hell you never come back. We're sad to see you go." We sang it over and over.

At that point, I felt sorry for Mr. Howard. Although he behaved like a child, perhaps we should have sucked it up and been a little patient with him. Maybe he had problems we didn't know about. However, I was sure glad he resigned.

Later I talked with Louie. I said, "What if the axel came off and it punctured the gas tank, then a spark ignited an explosion, the car burned, and Howie couldn't get out? We'd all be going up on manslaughter charges." That was all the pranks. For me, I was out of the prank business. But the story did not end there. A few months later my dad said, "Get the big chain. We have a job to do."

I said, "Dad, I took it to school." He asked why. I said, "We had a project." I was lucky he didn't ask, "What project?"

Then he asked, "Where is it now?"

I said, "Someone took it" (I'm glad he didn't ask, "Who took it?").

Then he said, "You'll have to go down to the Roy Co. and buy a new one."

Becoming a recovering prankster guaranteed I'd have a quieter and less nerve-wracking senior year coming up. I finally put behind me the "childish things."

(l-r) Bill, Louie Hardick, John McDonough

I felt very privileged to have had parents like the ones I had. They made a success out of what could have been a very negative marriage situation. If only kids facing the reality of divorce or of living in a single parent family could have had the role models I had.

My dad often instructed me, "Bill, do the extra, don't run with the crowd, and don't always play it safe." He also had many sayings that we heard regularly as we were growing up—"Any job worth doing is worth doing right," "If you start something, finish it." But there was one saying that he drummed into my head—"Fifteen minutes early, fifteen minutes late." That is if you work for someone, and he sets your hours, show up fifteen minutes early and stay fifteen minutes late.

When I graduated from Sussex High School in June of 1954, my dad wanted me to get a job off the farm. "You need experience from working for someone else," he said. So I found a job with Lawrence Yetter in the equipment rental and home oil delivery business. My hours of work were from eight a.m. to five p.m. So applying what my dad had taught me, I came to the site at seven forty in the morning and worked cleaning the yard and getting the equipment cleaned and lined up. I noticed that I was the only one there. At eight o'clock I would punch the clock, and at five o'clock I punched it again. Then I swept up and straightened the equipment again. Although four or five yard men were hired to work the yard, I realized that I was the only one who stayed late.

After two weeks working for Yetter's, Lawrence called me into his office. "I see that you are taking a real interest in your job and our company," he said. "How would you like to come out of the yard and drive a truck? It comes with a raise in pay and your own truck." Wow! I would do anything to get out of the yard—the work there was backbreaking. My father's words had paid off big-time. My job there, however, was short-lived—maybe three weeks in my new position. The Korean War was still going on, and not long after we graduated, several of my classmates and I got notices: "Join some branch of the service or you will be drafted into the Army in thirty days." Some of my friends and I decided to join the Marine Corps.

CHAPTER III

PARRIS ISLAND AND THE OBSTACLE COURSE

When ye shall have done all these things that are commanded of you, say, We are unprofitable servants; we have done that which it was our duty to do. (Luke 17:10, ASV).

I could write a book on the three months that I spent at Parris Island. It was an inhumane experience. I will go over some of the major events. I was attached to Platoon 370, which started with 125 men; when the punishment began many cried like babies for their mommies. They were all P.U.D'd out (psychologically unfit for duty.) At graduation, we ended up with seventy-five men. Our head drill instructor was Sgt. Womack, a real sadist. On his introduction to us, he stated, "I have a steel plate in my head from a hand grenade going off near my foxhole, two steel rods in my legs from jumping out of an airplane when my parachute only partially opened. And I have three broken ribs from hand-to-hand combat. But don't worry, I'll never ask you to do anything I haven't done."

He lived up to his words. Duck-walking in full packs and rifles on our backs in temperatures that hovered around a hundred degrees on the asphalt behind the barracks after the red flag had gone up. The red flag prohibited all physical activity. Only classroom instruction was permitted. Men were passing out and left lying in their own sweat. On a nearly weekly basis he would come into the barracks around three a.m., drunk, throw on the lights, made us stand at attention at the end of our bunks and proceed to beat up one or two recruits with his fists and his swagger stick, an eighteen-inch oak baton with a metal end used by drill instructors when marching troops. The beaten men would fall on the floor, some of them bleeding. Worst, Womack would then go to bed and leave us standing at attention for the rest of the night. One by one our platoon shrank. I don't know how I made it.

The worst incident occurred when we moved to the Quonset hut area before going to the rifle range. One evening Womack called us into ranks and to attention, and then he disappeared. Now, when you are at attention, you must look straight ahead, neither head nor eyes moving. Standing at attention for any length of time is very hard. Your legs weaken, your arms begin to sag, your neck stiffens, and you start to wobble. You want to move your head. Normally attention lasts for one or two minutes at most, and then you are called to "at ease." Then your feet could come apart, and your body relaxes. But before Womack could call "at ease" he had left and did not come back for half an hour. All of a sudden, Womack bolted into our ranks, flailing and swinging his swagger stick yelling "You turn your head! You turn your head!" His anger focused on one particular recruit in our squad. The end result of that was that the targeted recruit had three or four of his front teeth knocked out.

When Womack left, some of us urged him to go to sick bay, but he refused because he feared repercussions that would follow an investigation. This was a big mistake that would cost him his life. He was in our Quonset hut and couldn't stop the bleeding. When we woke up in the morning, he was as white as his sheet. His blood ran down his sheet and like a stream ran across the floor to a drain in the floor. And Sgt. Womack was nowhere to be seen. We called to our junior drill instructor, Sgt. Prebble, but it was too late. We were told he had no heartbeat.

The next day Sgt. Womack called a number of us into his room, one at a time. I was one. He asked, "Will you sign a paper saying the recruit fell over from heat exhaustion and injured his mouth on the steps leading to the hut?" With fear for my future and sweat on my brow, I said I could not sign it. He found three who would sign, and that's the way it went down.

We had no one we could talk to about the incident. Both other drill instructors knew exactly what happened. I was, however, a Roman Catholic and allowed to go to church on Sundays. I took the opportunity, and while in the confessional, I told the priest what had happened. Basically, he told me to keep my mouth shut. There was no one else to confide in.

These are only a few of the dehumanizing things that our platoon suffered. I could write several more chapters on Womack's insane treatment. We expected boot camp to be physically tough but not cruel. It did not make us Marines—it made us mad because of always being on edge and the fear of physical harm. We didn't perform well as a unit. This didn't bode well for Womack. We finished last in our performance testing. Sgt. Womack's drill instructor tour was over.

Graduation day, 9/25/54, Platoon 370, Parris Island
Sgt. Womack (center front, note "swagger stick" in left hand)

While I was at boot camp, I met Bob Hoppe, a man who would play a major part in my spiritual life in the future. We had survived the boot camp ordeal together and became best friends. Afterward, we both got transferred to Camp Lejeune in North Carolina for advanced infantry training. I met a Marine there who said he was part of Sgt. Womack's platoon that graduated just before our Platoon 370. He said that Womack got transferred to Camp Lejeune as an instructor. He informed me that a bunch of his buddies met Womack in a bar and a fight ensued out behind the building. They beat him up so bad that he died. The Marine said that everybody kept their mouths shut and there were no repercussions. The chickens had come home to roost. Justice had been done! But I felt no satisfaction in it.

We finished infantry training and Bob and I were transferred to Quantico, Virginia. Quantico was the location of officers' candidate school the way Parris Island was for first lieutenants. The duty was miserable—sleeping outside in a pup tent, hot summer nights and bitterly cold winter nights. We acted like the enemy to train officers in the field. When I couldn't take it anymore, I asked for a transfer to sea duty. I thought "At least I would have a warm bunk and a shower at night." I got my transfer but had to extend my enlistment an extra year.

Having seen the horrors of Nazism and experienced the rule of a sadist, I longed for a place of peace in a world of brutality. I was soon to learn why these things happened.

What a relief! Sea school for thirty days. I felt like a college student—classes, field trips to great ships. I learned that a ship is a different breed. It doesn't have a left or right; it has a port and starboard. It doesn't have a front and back; it has a bow and stern. It doesn't have walls; it has bulkheads. It doesn't have stairs; it has ladders. It doesn't have bathrooms; it has heads (I often wondered what relieving yourself has to do with a head).

It doesn't have a dining room; it has a mess hall. It doesn't accurately express what's served there; actually, the food was good. Now I could put some of the principles my father had taught me into practice.

Classes started at eight a.m. I would show up fifteen minutes early, get my materials ready before everybody else showed up. When classes were over at about four p.m., I would stick around, complete my notes, and straighten up the desks before going back to the barracks. All of my classmates would change into their greens and split to East Main Street in downtown Norfolk. East Main Street was known locally as Sin Strip for its bars and the availability of prostitutes. It was the place to go for sailors and Marines on liberty.

I wasn't a teetotaler and could have drunk some sailors under the table, but that lifestyle was not for me. On returning from my classes on the first day, I noticed a professional obstacle course right across from my barracks, so I would change into athletic gear and run the course every afternoon. Now, this course was about a quarter of a mile long and was used for competition between the services. I would run it one way and then the other way. The more I did, the better I got. I knew the angles to approach the walls, how to use the ropes to my advantage to get over the obstacles. There was a competition coming up, and after a month of running the course, I knew I could win. I didn't belong to a team. However, I could enter an open race at the end of their competition, but graduation from sea school was coming up, so I lost out on what I thought could be my big day.

The setting for our graduation was in a large hangar because it was raining. There were two companies of Marines graduating that day, about a hundred of us. With M-1 rifles on our shoulders and in our dress greens, we paraded in front of the grandstand and then formed open ranks for inspection. The base commandant spoke a few words and then inspected the troops. Following these activities, we were dismissed to a large bleacher area. There, each of us was called up in alphabetical order to receive our certificates of graduation from sea school and then get our ship assignments. "Pvt. Francisco to the *USS Forrestal*," "Pvt. James to the *USS Roosevelt*." I had a long wait since I was down the order with Wesniewski and Zabriski. My heart was in my throat as I contemplated what ship I would get. Where would I spend the next three years? Finally, I heard my name called. "Pvt. Spanjer, Com. Cru. Div. Six. What! Why was it not a ship? Did I get a rowboat or something? I took my certificate, saluted the commandant, and walked backed to my seat. I was seated near an instructor who was standing at the end of the bleachers and asked him, "What ship did I get?"

"You are attached to Commander Cruiser Division Six as part of the admiral's staff." Wow! I couldn't believe it! An admiral!

The admiral for whom I would work was Rear Admiral Laurence R. Daspit, a man I discovered to be of great integrity, morality, and character. I would be his assistant, driver, aide, and security. We were assigned to the *USS Boston*. I was put in charge of five Marines who were assigned to the admiral and his staff. We operated independently from other Marines on the ship. I had a brand new '56 Chevy sedan to transport the admiral, an open gangway liberty pass, carried a .45 caliber automatic pistol with twenty-one rounds of ammunition at all times. I was the envy of all the sailors and Marines on board our ship mainly for the open gangway pass—they had to get special permission to leave the ship. I could come and go at any time. This would cause me backlash and grief often.

ARMED FORCES LIBERTY PASS	SERVICE USMC		DATE ISSUED 5-28-57	
LAST NAME—FIRST NAME—MIDDLE INITIAL SPANJER, William H.			CARD NO. - - - - -	
SERVICE NO. 1477140		GRADE—RATE SGT		
ORGANIZATION—INSTALLATION—BASE Flag Allowance, COMCRUDIV 6				
TIME LIMITS None (OPEN GANGWAY)				
SIGNATURE AND GRADE OF ISSUING OFFICER J.W. STONER, LTJG, USN				
DD(N)-345 1 April 1950			16—63060-1 GPO	

"Open Gangway" Pass

A friend once asked me, "How did you get this great job?" My mind went back to graduation day at sea school. Before leaving, I thanked my instructors, and when I said goodbye to the sergeant major, I asked him how I had gotten the assignment. He said, "Your instructors told me that you always showed up early to class before the rest of your buddies to go over your notebook. And my office is located right across from the obstacle course. Every afternoon, I saw you running the course when others were in slop chutes (bars) in Norfolk. I had one assignment open for the top position, and I gave it to you." Wow! My father's advice had paid off a second time. Big-time.

Jesus reminds us in Luke 17 that when we do all that we are expected to do, we are not done yet. "Fifteen minutes early, fifteen minutes late" or going beyond what you are required to do will pay big rewards in our spiritual and everyday lives. It is the key to success. My success with Lawrence Yetter and now at the obstacle course stuck with me through the years, especially in business, and later in ministry. My dad's advice was well taken:

"Do the extra and go against the crowd; don't always play it safe." In other words, no risk, no gain.

The six Marines assigned to Admiral Daspit's Flag Allowance
(Spanjer, far right)

CHAPTER IV

BOB HOPPE AND THE USS BOSTON

Verily, verily I say unto thee, Except a man be born again, he cannot see the kingdom of God (John 3:3, KJV).

Therefore if any man be in Christ, he is a new creature: old things are passed away; behold, all things are become new (II Corinthians 5:17, KJV).

I was proud to walk the decks of the *USS Boston*. I transferred there while it was in dry dock in the U.S. naval shipyard at Philadelphia. The ship, which had a complement of about 1,500 men, was over 673 feet long, seventy-one feet wide and displaced over 17,000 tons of water. It had taken part in some of the fiercest battles of World War II in the South Pacific. From

USS Boston
Guided Missile Cruiser

December 1943 the *Boston* had fought in the battles of the Carolinas, the invasion of Saipan, the Philippines, the landings at Okinawa, and even the bombardment of Japan itself. The ship had over ten battle stars, and hundreds of men had given their lives on her decks in these and other battles. I felt as though I walked on sacred planks.

On our first shakedown cruise to Guantanamo Bay in Cuba ("Gitmo" as the sailors called it), we participated in fleet exercises, testing out the accuracy of our new Terrier, surface-to-air guided missiles. On one such trial run, we had some congressmen and Department of Defense officials on board for a demonstration of what the Terriers could do. A B-17 drone was launched from Norfolk Naval Air Station. It flew at 35,000 feet. As we awaited its arrival, everyone on the bridge got very tense. If this demonstration didn't come off successfully, funds for future guided-missile-program ships would be lost. All eyes were fixed overhead. The problem was that all the spotters had binoculars which limit your view to a very small area. All was quiet as the watchers scanned the skies. I held my post standing behind the admiral on the open bridge when I saw it. "Admiral," I said, "I see the plane at eleven o'clock off the port bow." The drone was just coming out from behind some high clouds.

The admiral said over the ship's speaker. "Does anyone see it yet?"

"No, sir," was the reply.

"Well, my orderly spotted it with the naked eye off the port bow at eleven o'clock." I was quite embarrassed by this announcement as it was broadcast throughout the ship and consequently made myself scarce with the crew for the next few days to avoid any backlash.

The missile launchers jolted and locked into position. The weapons officer said, "Launch when ready." The first Terrier roared off the missile platform, followed fifteen seconds later by the launch of a second missile. The missile hit the B-17 in the middle of its fuselage; the drone broke in two. The bigger half, wings and engines fell wide and separately. I could see the second missile veer sharply to the right to attack the larger portion of the plane as it fell. Wow! I was impressed with this new state-of-the-art warfare. The congressmen were equally impressed, and the Navy got the funds to complete the *Boston's* sister ship, the *USS Canberra*.

As we prepared for our first six-month deployment to the Mediterranean, one of my Marines transferred off the ship for medical reasons—I needed a replacement. On impulse, I talked to the gunny sergeant of our Marine detachment aboard ship. "Gunny, I know a good Marine who would like to transfer to our ship. His name is Bob Hoppe." He said he would see what he could do.

In November 1956, two weeks before we left Port Norfolk, Bob walked up the gangplank of the *Boston*. We were united again! And the admiral's staff was now complete.

Now, Bob was one tough Marine. He had made it through the Womack saga, could drink anyone under the table, and fight at the drop of an argument, which he thoroughly enjoyed. One night, when it was lightly raining, Bob had liberty, and he wanted to go to Norfolk's East Main Street. This strip was known by sailors and Marines for its bars, ladies of the night, and a rough local crowd. Knowing that I needed to take the admiral's car to get his newspaper, Bob asked me if I could drop him off at this infamous street. Uh-oh! The admiral's car could not be seen anywhere near East Main Street—I could lose my position. So I dropped Bob off a few blocks away and went off to complete my task. Afterward, I returned the car to the ship and went to sleep.

Now, we slept in bunks called racks, three high, about two feet apart. I slept in the middle rack and Bob slept on the bottom one. About 0400, Bob was shaking me to wake up. "Wake up, wake up!"

I said, "What's the matter?"

He said, "I got saved tonight!"

I said, "Saved from what?"

"From my sins," Bob said.

"Bob," I muttered, "you are drunk. Let me get you into your bunk." Then I noticed that he dropped into a kneeling position, so I went back to sleep. A few hours later when reveille sounded, Bob was still in that same position. After he got to his feet, we got dressed and prepared for duty that day. Later I asked Bob what had happened to him the night before.

It seems that after I dropped him off, he was walking toward East Main Street. He came upon a group of young people standing on a corner. As was his habit, Bob got into an argument, this time about the Bible! It was a book that neither Bob nor I had ever read. The argument could not be settled on the corner, so one of the teens suggested that Bob go with them to see their pastor who lived right down the street. Of course, Bob who thought he knew everything, went, determined he would set this pastor straight.

Four hours later, Bob found himself on his knees accepting Jesus Christ as his savior. The pastor had explained to Bob that although he might be a "good" person, he had disobeyed the commandments of God, thereby creating a personal debt that he owed to God. This debt, if left unpaid would, at his death, have to be paid by Bob himself. The consequences would be a second death and hell for eternity. But, the pastor explained, if Bob accepted the payment that Jesus had made for him by His death on the cross, if he would repent and ask Jesus to forgive him of his debt, the Lord would save him from these consequences. All of Bob's arguments failed him. He accepted Jesus Christ and was saved. And all of this is explained in the third chapter of the Gospel of John. From that day forward I never heard another swear word come out of Bob's mouth. He never again drank, fought, or got into an argument. It was truly an instant conversion and transformation.

The next day our ship pulled out for a six-month deployment to the Mediterranean and the Near East. We were on our way to join the Sixth Fleet in the Mediterranean. After arriving, we joined the *USS Forrestal*, the first nuclear-powered aircraft carrier and her strike group for war exercises during which we used four of our forty-six Terrier guided missiles.

Bob Hoppe with one of two Terrier missile launchers on the USS Boston

Bob had no support in his new found faith—no pastor to confide in or learn from, no other Christian with whom to fellowship. All he had was a small New Testament that we had received at Parris Island. I recommended to Bob that since he had "found religion" that he should become a Roman Catholic. After all, that was the true church.

Now it just so happened that our ship's chaplain was a Roman Catholic priest. So Bob, genuinely searching for Biblical knowledge, scheduled several meetings with Father Martin in the evenings. One night I asked Bob how it was going. He said, "Bill, I don't think Father Martin believes the Bible."

"What?" I said, "Of course he believes the Bible. He's a priest in the Catholic Church!"

So Bob and I sat down and went over his concerns. Bob said the priest told him that he should come to confession so his sins can be given absolution (forgiven). But Bob said, "I just read in Mark 2:10 that Jesus is the only one that can forgive sins." He said that he had just read in the book of I John that if we confess our sins to Jesus, He would forgive us our sins and cleanse us from all unrighteousness (I John 1:9, KJV). Bob said, "I asked Father Martin why we had to confess our sins to a priest? Father Martin said that the priest stands between God and man." Bob said to me that he read in I Timothy 2:5 that there is one mediator between God and man who is Jesus Christ.

The next night, Bob came to me with a worried look on his face. I asked what happened. "Father Martin gave me a rosary with a printed prayer to Mary entitled 'Hail Mary' and said to say this prayer for each bead." Bob said the priest said that prayers to Mary may lessen the time you may spend in purgatory, which Bob said is a very bad place. Bob told me that he had almost read all of the New Testament and Jesus, Paul and the other writers never wrote about prayers to Mary or a place called purgatory. Certainly, if these issues were as important as Father Martin said, Jesus and the other apostles would have said something about them. But there's nothing. Then Bob said that if purgatory is a place we go after we die, why did Jesus say to the thief on the cross who was crucified next to him, 'This day you shall be with me in paradise'?

I began to ponder why these doctrines which are so prominent in the Catholic Church not in the Bible. Are not the Gospels and the New Testament writers the source of our Christian faith? Why are these doctrines not in it? This dilemma stayed in my mind for some time until I found the answer about a year later.

Our deployment in the Mediterranean continued during we stopped at the port of Naples for liberty. At that time, the admiral wanted to tour the countryside, so I took the admiral, and we visited little towns and villages in Northern Italy. Upon arriving back at the ship, the admiral gave me a day off, and Bob and I went on liberty together. For two packs of cigarettes, we rented a motor scooter and drove up to the top of Mount Vesuvius and later visited Pompeii.

That evening, Bob and I got the hankering for a real Italian pizza, so we dove into an authentic little restaurant and we licked our chops for a real Italian pizza. When it came, we were shocked! It was a round piece of uncooked dough, with four slices of tomato and two slices of cold mozzarella cheese on top. We were outraged. Give me a New York dirty water pizza any day. We left hungry and dejected. But despite this, we'd had a great experience in Naples.

When we returned from our first deployment to the Mediterranean, Bob and I had time off to visit Washington and the Marine Corps Memorial.

Bill (on right) with Bob Hoppe
Marine Corps Memorial, Washington D.C.

CHAPTER V

TROUBLE ON LAND AND SEA

When peace like a river attendeth my way, When sorrows like sea billows roll—Whatever my lot, thou hast taught me to say, It is well, it is well with my soul.
— Horatio Spafford, "It is Well with My Soul," 1873

After my experience with the Lord on the last deployment, I knew God had something planned for me. I wanted to go to a college where I could study the Bible and get some of my theological questions answered. However, I still had over a year left in my enlistment. It was difficult, but I had to stick it out. Because of the course of events over the next few years, I needed divine protection to stay on track to become a true disciple.

When we came back from our Mediterranean deployment in the spring of 1957, Admiral Daspit transferred his flag to the *USS Canberra*, the sister ship of the *USS Boston*. At that time Bob Hoppe stayed with the *Boston* and became part of the Marine detachment there. By the time that the current deployment was over, I believe Bob had spoken to the entire crew, including the admiral, about the gospel.

On the *Canberra*, we set out for another Mediterranean deployment in the fall of '57. Before going over the difficulties of that trip, let me relate the story leading up to that deployment. My dad had always had a motorcycle around the farm when I was growing up. It was a big bike—an Indian Chief. I can remember riding on the back often to make a run to the local country store to get food supplies. These consisted of bread and cans of baked beans, which we ate cold because there was no stove or electricity in the farmhouse at that time. Later, after the war, when we moved onto the farm, Dad modernized the house with electricity, water, and centralized heat. In 1953, when I was an eleventh grader, the family of a classmate of mine was selling their old motorcycle, a 1934 Harley Davidson 74. By that time, I was a motorcycle addict. The bike was newly restored, painted black and orange with a square gas tank, three-speed transmission, and a shifting knob on the left side of the gas tank. In addition, it had a left foot suicide clutch, so called because a cyclist had to take his hand off the left handlebar to shift the bike. Riders would often lose control when shifting in traffic and other closely confined situations. Even on the open road shifting could prove dangerous. Dad agreed to go look at it, and he bought it for me. It had so much more power than the Cushman motor scooter I had had before that. At first, I drove the Harley in first and second gear, as I was nervous to go into third. After two weeks of practice and proving to my dad that I could handle the big Harley, he let me drive it to school. After three years of hitchhiking home from sports practices each day, I finally had my own transportation. When the Marine Corps came knocking, my dad sold the Harley because of pressure from my stepmom who didn't want him anywhere near it.

When we came back from our first Mediterranean deployment, we were told that the ship would be in Port Norfolk for two or three months before her next deployment and I got the biking itch again. So I went to the Harley Davidson dealer, and with the help of Household Financial Corporation, I bought a brand new Harley 74 FLH with hydro-glide, a windshield, buddy seat molded saddlebags. It was a beauty—deep maroon with white accent stripes. It had a hand clutch and a left foot shifting—no more risk of a suicide crash! For the next four months, Bob and I went everywhere on it.

The admiral got transferred to the *Boston's* sister ship, the *USS Canberra*, and just before we were to ship out, the admiral told me to take a long weekend. That was on a Wednesday, and the *Canberra* was due to leave port on the following Monday morning at 0800 hours. There was plenty of time for me to make a trip back home to the farm. Now if you take the Cape Charles ferry across to the Chesapeake Bay, then up Route 13 you can avoid Wilmington, Virginia, Washington D.C. and Baltimore. I was on the ferry at about 1600 hours (four p.m.). It was about 375 miles from Norfolk to the farm in Branchville, New Jersey, about a six or seven-hour drive if there was not heavy traffic and I got home just before midnight. I had a great time with my family, milked some cows, drove a John Deere, and saw some friends. But Sunday came quickly. By 1500 hours (three p.m.) the sky started to cloud over. I had a lengthy goodbye because I knew that with this cruise coming up, I would not see my family for about five months.

By the time I got to Trenton, New Jersey, rain had begun to fall, although it was light at first. I had rain gear in my saddlebags. The rain began to fall more heavily. I still had two hundred miles to go to reach the ferry at Cape Charles. After going through Salisbury, Maryland, the rain intensified into a storm—wind gusts were so strong that I had a hard time keeping the bike on the road. I had to slow down to thirty miles an hour and the rain was driving me sideward on the road, and I still had a hundred miles left to go. It seemed like forever, but I finally spotted the lights of the Cape Charles lighthouse. "Ten minutes to go," I thought, "and I'll be on the ferry—high, dry and warm." As I approached the ramp, however, I saw that the gate was down, and cars were piling up. "What's going on?" I questioned the driver of a nearby car. He answered that ferry service to Norfolk had been shut down due to the storm. What?! This couldn't be happening. It was 200 miles back to Wilmington and another 170 miles through Baltimore, Washington, D.C. and Richmond, Virginia to get around the Chesapeake Bay to Norfolk.

I checked the time. It was 0100 hours (1 a.m.). If I could average fifty miles an hour, the trip would take me about eight hours. Our ship was due to leave port at 0800. I knew that I couldn't do fifty mph because of the wind gusts, but I had to try anyway. For a Marine, missing your ship is a court-martial offense, so I started out. I had to repeat again the same miles that I had covered on my way from the farm.

After about 200 miles I got a break when the wind let up. I got onto Route 95 and headed for Baltimore. Thinking that maybe I could make up time, I pushed that Harley to eighty and ninety mph. I raced through the gate at the Norfolk Naval Shipyard at 0900 hours, tore down the docking road to the pier where the *Canberra* hopefully was still tied. It was there. But as I drove down the pier, I noticed that the foreward gangway was already gone, and a crane was about to remove the aft gangway. "Wait, wait!" I yelled. The Officer of the Deck saw and heard me, and the cranes stopped. But what would I do with my motorcycle? I spotted sailors handling the ropes attached to the ship, and I hollered, "Can you take my bike to the Harley dealer?" They yelled back that they would, and putting down my kickstand, I dismounted. Now, after riding 680 miles, I could hardly walk, much less run, but I gave it my best effort, sloshing up the gangway in my soaking clothing. Saluting the Officer of the Deck, I said, "Permission to come aboard, sir."

He replied, "Granted." And then he added, "You're out of uniform, Marine."

"Yessir," I answered. "I'll get changed right away, sir." But I said it with relief. I had just made it. And I knew that God had had something to do with getting me back on time and safely. He will give His angels charge over thee and keep thee in all thy ways, the psalmist writes.

The ordeal was not quite over yet. I had twenty minutes to shower, get into uniform, and be on the bridge with the admiral for departure. When I arrived there, Admiral Daspit asked me, "Did you get back okay?"

"By the skin of my teeth, sir," I replied, and he answered that he had given the captain permission to delay departure one hour because it was reported to him that the Cape Charles ferry had been canceled due to the weather. It was clear that God's angel works in mysterious ways and I would need Him even more on this deployment. This deployment would take us to Italy and Spain and to joint war exercises with the Sixth Fleet.

On this deployment, we docked at the Firth of Clyde in Scotland. The car was put ashore for me to take the admiral to a conference. The admiral gave me two hours to practice driving on the left side of the road. He wanted to be sure that I did not make a mistake with him in the car, but two hours was not really enough time. After a short visit, he told me that we were going to Portsmouth, England. He did not want to put the car back on board, so he gave me some money, told me to drive the car to London and said, "I will see you in ten days." Wow! So I took my fellow Marine with me, and we visited the University of Edinburgh, saw a number of castles and farms while working our way south. We got to London and had two days before the *Canberra* was due to dock in Portsmouth. We took time to see the sights in there. The place that stood out in my mind the best was our visit to Westminster Cathedral—I'll talk more about this visit in a later chapter. After our tour of London, we proceeded to Portsmouth to join the *Canberra* and continue on to our Mediterranean deployment. We once again joined the Sixth Fleet for war exercises.

Two weeks later we were assigned liberty in the port of Barcelona, Spain. It was a beautiful city, and the crew was grateful to get some time off the ship. It was a Friday when we were in port that the admiral called me in and told me that he had to go to a NATO meeting in Brussels the next day. He told me to bring the car alongside in an hour and take him to the Naval Air Station for a flight that evening.

As we awaited the plane he was to board, the admiral said, "I should be back later Sunday. Stay in touch with the Officer of the Day for my arrival time."

I saluted the admiral and replied, "Yes, sir." And I waited until he was on the plane and it had flown out of sight. I had Saturday off, and Bob and I had planned a day and night of activities in Barcelona! But our plans were foiled when Lt. J.G. Michelson called me in early Saturday morning and informed me that the admiral's chief of staff wanted me to take the senior staff out on the town that evening. "Have the car ready at 1600 hours (four o'clock) sharp." There went my only day off in that port.

I had the car at the officers' gangway at 1600 hours and waited until 1700 hours when they came down the gangway. There were five of them, the chief of staff and four other senior officers. They all piled in; it was very cramped inside the '56 Chevy. We drove around for about an hour and a half, as they wanted to see the sights of Barcelona. At about 1830 they decided that they were ready for dinner. After arguing with a police officer for fifteen minutes on where we could find the best place to eat, we got directions to a little restaurant in North Barcelona. The men went in, and I waited for about two hours until they came out, all of them a little tipsy.

Next, they wanted to go to a bar someone had recommended.

Right then I knew I was in big trouble. I drove there, and they all clambered out, and I waited for another three hours. But this time when they came out, what a mess! Their uniform jackets were open, their ties were on backward, and they had to carry one of the officers to the car. As they piled in again, Lt. Michelson handed me a little card with an address written on it. "Take us there," he ordered. Well, I didn't know where I was going, and I didn't speak Spanish, but at last, I found the place—a dingy hotel. The men, without saying a word to me, got out of the car and walked into the building. About two hours later, they came out in even worse shape than they went in. Uniforms were unbuttoned, hats were on sideways—they reeked of alcohol and cheap perfume. They stumbled out, one officer lay across the trunk, and others leaned against the car. It took me nearly ten minutes to get them inside the car, where one of the officers vomited in the backseat!

I was totally embarrassed—people had seen the entire thing, and I was embarrassed for the Navy and for America that supposedly responsible senior officers should behave in such a way. When I got them back to the ship, the Officer of the Day was not happy with their condition. I felt good inside that someone else felt as disgusted as I was.

To compound the situation, I had gotten to know these officers. Coming often to their compartments to summon them to meetings with the admiral, I saw pictures of their wives and children on their desks. I also saw their entire families come on board to welcome them after long tours at sea. What were these men thinking about? How could they face their wives and children after this episode of unfaithfulness and disgrace! It was confirmed in my mind again that the heart of man is desperately wicked. When he is far away and thinks nobody's looking, he will allow his true nature to come out.

With all of the activity of that day, I hadn't eaten since breakfast, and it was too late to go to the mess hall. Normally, when I was with the admiral driving on tours, when protocol allowed, the admiral would invite me to go to dinner and lunch with him, which was a great honor for a sergeant in the Marine Corps, and I respected him for it.

Well, that Sunday morning found me on the pier next to the ship, trying to get the admiral's car cleaned out. Even after scrubbing and scrubbing, I was unable to get the smell of vomit and alcohol out. Willing to try whatever I could, I went to my locker on the ship and found a bottle of Old Spice aftershave. I splashed it around the inside of the car. It seemed like a good idea, but I think it made the car smell worse, like rotten sweet-and-sour chicken. Not long after, the Officer of the Day called down to me, "I got a message that the admiral is due back at 1130." What? I knew I could never get the foul smell out of the car by then.

I was waiting at the field when the admiral's plane landed. "Did you have a good flight, sir?" I asked. He replied that it was a little bumpy as I opened his door. He got in, and when I went around the car to get behind the wheel, he asked, "What happened to my car?" That was a direct question that required an answer. I wanted to say that the garbage crew mistook our car for a dumpster. But his words meant that I had to tell the story as it was. So I did.

The admiral heard my story of the previous night, listening calmly. When I was done, he said, "When we get back to the ship, tell my chief of staff that I want to see him immediately."

Well, the cat was out of the bag. I ran up the ladder to the chief of staff's cabin. My orderly was standing guard duty outside of his door when I arrived. "The admiral wants to see the captain right away," I stated.

"He's sleeping," was the orderly's reply.

"What," I exclaimed. "It's 1300 in the afternoon! Go wake him up!"

The orderly went in, but was back in a few minutes. "I can't wake him. He has a bad hangover."

"The admiral wants to see him now!" I said. "Let's go in and get him up."

Together we entered the chief of staff's private bedroom. It was very dark. I knew right there that if the admiral did not have my back, it would be all over for me.

After about five minutes of shaking and a few slaps, the captain began to regain consciousness. When he came to, I told his orderly to give him the message, and I slipped out quickly before he saw me. I didn't want him to think that I was getting squealer's revenge. I disappeared after that.

Afterward I talked about this episode with several Marines, and their opinion was "They're just boys away from home. Let them have a good time."

My response was "Disgraceful good times may have bad consequences." Sure enough, I was told that the chief of staff was relieved of command when our deployment was over. The rest of the group got official reprimands for behavior unbecoming officers in the Navy and disorderly conduct—very serious offenses if you are competing with other officers who are looking for promotions.

I learned a very important lesson from Admiral Daspit because of that episode that affected my approach to business and ministry. If you want to be successful in business or pleasing to God in your ministry, you must not overlook any violation of the rules. The consequences may vary depending on the degree of the violation, but everything must come into the light. I have lost many employees and even more students in my ministries, sometimes at a great financial loss, but this principle has been honored and blessed by the Lord.

Our deployment in the Mediterranean continued. It was on this deployment that I would get myself into big trouble. In arguing with a sailor in charge of the deck with the admiral's car on it, I refused to obey him because what he demanded would have damaged the car's windshield. If the windshield were damaged, where was I to get a new one for a '56 Chevy in Naples, Italy? Well, he wrote me up for disobedience of a direct order, which required that I be brought up to Captain's Mast. It was to be held on the bridge in three days. If I was found guilty, I could lose a stripe, making me lose my job with the admiral—only a sergeant was eligible to be his driver and personal assistant. The crew was ecstatic. They all needled me as I walked around the ship. "You're gonna lose your open gangway pass! You're gonna get busted!"

So I went to Captain's Mast, represented by Lieutenant J.G. Stoner of the admiral's staff. I knew the captain as I did some "fill-in" work for him when we were in port. But that didn't make any difference. "Guilty of disobeying an order" was his pronouncement. Now I awaited my sentence. "Suspended bust," said the captain. Suspended bust meant that I didn't lose a stripe, but if I had one more mishap on the rest of the deployment, the loss of a stripe would be automatic. The crew was furious. They had been hoping for vengeance and tried to force me to take that one false step.

When off duty and walking down the deck, I would hear a boson yell, "Don't take another step on my clean deck." I would freeze in midair, do an about face, and get out of there. Waiting for about fifteen minutes on the chow line. I finally got to pick up a tray, the mess chief stated, "Go to the back of the line," and I began another fifteen to twenty-minute wait. When I was finally able to grab another tray, the chief said, "The mess hall is closed. Try again tomorrow." And this scene was repeated the next day. None of my buddy Marines were able to remove food from the mess hall so they could not help me, and to make the situation worse, there were no vending machines on board. After three days without food, I was beginning to get weak, but knowing that they wanted me to blow my stack enabled me to keep my cool.

Around the fourth day, when getting some papers signed, Admiral Daspit asked me how everything was going since the Mast. I only told him that the crew was shunning me and preventing me from eating for four days, but I wanted to say that my bellybutton was kissing my backbone. I had no idea what the admiral would do. I did not want him to issue an order, which would solve my problem but would make me look like a crybaby. He did not say a thing as we shuffled through some more paperwork. He told me to sit down. Now an enlisted man is never allowed to sit down in the presence of a senior officer. But it was an order, and so I sat down. He buzzed for someone on the phone, and his private chef came in. "Sergeant Spanjer is going to come to my galley. You arrange the times and prepare him a meal from my menu." The chef answered, "Yes, Sir," and that's the way it was. I smiled, thanked the admiral, and went on my way. No one could figure out why I seemed so happy and well-fed. I was eating filet mignon and eggs benedict while the crew was eating "shit on a shingle." Only servicemen can appreciate what I am talking about.

When we returned to the States, we tied up alongside our sister ship the *USS Boston* in Norfolk harbor. It was a welcomed sight to see my friend Bob Hoppe waving to me from the decks of the Boston. I was very glad to get off the *Canberra* and one evening Bob and I got into a deep discussion and wanted to be able to continue it in privacy. Everyone around us was playing cards, kidding around, and I said, "Hey, Bob. The admiral's car is tied down on the O2 level. Let's go and sit in the back seat." And so we did.

After talking casually for about thirty minutes, we began discussing the Bible. We read passages and talked for about two hours, then prayed together and went back to our compartments. That conversation changed my life. I came to realize two important spiritual facts. First, Bob opened my eyes to the fact that God wants a personal relationship with me, not an organizational one. Like most Catholics, I had depended on the church to meet my spiritual needs and ultimately secure my salvation. We were encouraged to pray for ourselves but were also taught that we needed to follow proscribed steps to receive merit or at least a pathway to heaven after a stint in purgatory. Bob pointed out that Scripture emphasizes a personal relationship between our God and us. Jesus said, "I have called you friends" (John 15:15, KJV). Friends, he pointed out, indicates a close personal relationship. Further, we are to address God as "our Father," and the Apostle Paul even goes on to say that we are sons of the Father, able to cry Abba, Father, personally. Thus Scripture assures us, we are heirs of our Father, which means we have eternal life through Jesus Christ as an inheritance (Galatians 4:5, Romans 8:17). Consequently, we can come boldly and directly to our Father's throne (Hebrews 4:16). There is no intermediary, no purgatory, no prayers to Mary or the saints mentioned in the Bible. The Catholic Douay version of the Bible has the same Gospels as the King James. Why are these doctrines not mentioned? I now had found that the most important thing in my life was that I could have this personal relationship with God. The Scriptures allowed me to take an end run around the sacramental system of the church and embrace God, Christ, and the

Holy Spirit personally, freely, and totally, as important as some of the sacraments are.

Secondly, I learned that night from Scripture that the Roman Catholic Church does not believe the gospel. The gospel according to the New Testament says that we have right standing with God (justification) not by merit, not by our own deeds, or by keeping the sacramental system, not by our prayers to the saints, no matter how earnest they are, but by faith in Jesus Christ alone. Paul the Apostle tells us that we are saved from the consequences of our sins which Jesus himself describes as everlasting punishment and a fire that never shall be quenched by grace through faith (Matthew 25:41). According to the Catholic Church, purgatory is not a peaceful place. The Apostle Paul reminds us in Scripture that those who have a personal relationship with God are justified by their faith and have peace with God through our Lord Jesus Christ. "Being therefore justified by faith, we have peace with God through one Lord Jesus Christ" (Romans 5:1, ASV). I am thankful for that night in the back seat of the admiral's car. I confessed my sins, verbally, repented, and embraced Jesus Christ as my personal savior by faith in Him alone.

The admiral called me in one day and said, "I have to go to a conference in Washington. Pack for two overnights."

"Yes sir," I replied. "I know the routes real good." He put me up in the same hotel that he was staying in and I thought, "If my compartment buddies could see me now." The next surprise that I had was when the admiral invited me to have dinner with him. Now I had eaten meals with him when touring the Spanish and Italian countryside, but this was Washington, D.C. Sergeants are not supposed to be seen dining with admirals, especially in an autocratic setting with other officers observing. The admiral was dressed in his uniform, which displayed his campaign ribbons. He was an acclaimed submarine skipper of the

Tinosa serving in the South Pacific during World War II. Then Commander Daspit and the crew of the *Tinosa* are credited with sinking thousands of tons of Japanese supply and troop ships in the war. He was noted for saving a Mark V torpedo and bringing it home for examination after a number of them misfired, bouncing off the hulls of Japanese ships. I watched him over the years, observed him in many tense and difficult situations. I respected him very much. I hoped I would not embarrass him in this very public and formal setting.

I wore my "dress-down blues" which consisted of blue pants with the red stripe down the side of the legs (which represented the blood shed by Marines in their many wars), a tropical khaki shirt with tie and appropriate ribbons.

Now to the point of this story. At that dinner, the admiral told me that his assignment with the Sixth Fleet was about to end. His new assignment would be with the Pacific Command and would take him to Hawaii, and would last two years before his retirement. "Do you want to go with me?" he asked. And then he added, "I am very impressed with your ability and dedication to your duty as a Marine. I would like to get you an appointment to Annapolis or to NOCS (Naval Officers Candidate School)". I could hardly contain myself—me, a farm kid from New Jersey offered a two-year stint in Hawaii and the possibility of becoming a Marine Corps officer! I nearly choked on my food. The admiral continued, "When we get back to Norfolk, I am going to give you a ten-day leave. Talk this all over with your family and let me know when you get back." If I chose to accept his offer, I would have to extend my enlistment for at least two years, and I wanted to go to college as soon as I could.

Further compounding the problem, I had grown to love the admiral's family. He and his wife had two children, a boy and a girl of about four and five years respectively. I had spent many hours when in port helping them with tasks when moving and on weekends.

Well, I found myself on that Harley once again pounding along on the 375-mile ride home. As I remember, it was a cold early spring morning, and somewhere on Route 13 headed toward Salisbury, MD, a sailor passed me in his car with his arm out the window, radio and heater on, leaning back in his seat with all of the comforts of home. I was cold, rain had started to fall, I couldn't lean back, and I had no radio. I decided right there to sell this motorcycle and get a car.

It was a great ten-day leave. My enlistment would be over in July. I had several talks with my dad about the decision I had to make. Dad never liked to give advice to anyone. He said at one point, "They never take it so, why give it?" However, at the end of that week, he said, "Bill, sometimes you have to choose the more difficult but better choice over the more enjoyable good," meaning college and the rigors of study over the beaches of Hawaii.

That next week, I had the most difficult meeting in my life. I had to tell Admiral Daspit, the man respected above every man I had met (except my dad), no thank you. I was sick, and my voice trembled. But the admiral was gracious. He said, "Sergeant, I support you in whatever is best for you."

Well, the admiral went to Hawaii, and I headed to Lakehurst Naval Air Station in New Jersey to await discharge.

As my tour in the USMC was coming to an end, I thought to myself what a rich and wonderful privilege it was to serve this great man. I thanked God that He gave me a father that taught me fifteen minutes early and fifteen minutes late. "Don't go with the crowd. Do more than required for your boss. Go the extra mile for your boss. Do the right thing—it always pays off." To my readers, I would remind them of the words of Jesus: "He who has ears, let him hear."

Rear Admiral Lawrence R. Daspit, Commander, Cruiser Division 6

CHAPTER VI

MONKEY ON MY BACK

There is therefore now no condemnation to them that are in Christ Jesus. For the law of the Spirit of life in Christ Jesus made me free from the law of sin and of death (Romans 8:1-2, ASV).

I want to say a couple of things at the outset of this chapter. First, I have observed that when God, by His pure grace, opens the eyes of certain people and gives them faith to believe and trust Him, the conversion is sometimes instantaneous and often dramatic. When people are "made alive" (the Apostle Paul's description of being born again—Ephesians 2:1-5) there is often an immediate change of lifestyle and commitment to the future. Such was the example of Bob Hoppe. For me, who had never smoked, swore, chewed, or went with girls who did, my conversion was not such a dramatic event. It was real, of course, but the commitment to the Kingdom of God and proclaiming the gospel had not yet been fully realized. I had begun a process, and I wandered a bit, but I believe that God in His sovereignty had me under His wings. Unbeknownst to me, God guided me with His hand over a number of years to come.

Another important truth became clear to me as I looked back at this time in my life. Although we deviate at times and wander off to follow our own path, when God calls us back to His plans and ultimate purposes for our lives, He often uses the experiences and lessons learned in the course of our deviation to benefit our calling. In my case, those lessons and experiences were essential for the future task God had for me. Humanly speaking I could not have accomplished the ministry He had for me without these experiences.

I was honorably discharged from the Marine Corps in July 1958, went home, worked on the farm, and continued my job with Lawrence Yetter.

I had two great mentors at that time—Pastor Carl Luthman and an elder in his church, Don Castner. Don became a close friend and eventually a member of my Board of Directors.

Although I had the G.I. Bill for my education, it would only pay about eighty percent of the cost for four years of college. So I worked and saved my money with this goal in mind. To further complicate my plans, my father presented me with two offers. First, he would give me the farm if I would take two years at ag school, or he said I could take over Spanjer Brothers if I would go for two years to a business college. Wow! I was only twenty-five and had three amazing offers. I would have loved a tour in Hawaii, loved farming, and loved business. What would I choose to do? At that time, I was reading a book titled *Jungle Pilot* that recounted the experiences of missionaries Nate Saint and Jim Elliot as they tried to reach the Huaorani people of Ecuador with the truth of the gospel. It was an exciting and intriguing book, and one statement by Saint, recalling the famous poem by C.T. Studd stayed in my mind for weeks. He said, "Only one life 'twill soon be past. Only what's done for Christ will last." My mind was made up. I respectfully told my dad that I wanted to pursue a Biblical education; I knew that he was disappointed because he had no one else in the family to take over these two businesses. Ironically, I almost found myself in a similar situation years later.

In that same year, many churches in our area came together

to sponsor a countywide Billy Graham crusade with a guest speaker named Leighton Ford, a very powerful evangelist. His lead man who came to organize the campaign and teach counseling courses was Forrest Layman, a senior at Columbia Bible College in South Carolina today known as Columbia International University. We became good friends during the crusade, and he strongly encouraged me to register at CBC. And I did, entering for the second semester in the winter of 1960.

Now I don't want to bore the reader with my college experiences, but I would like to mention a couple of discoveries I made at the two colleges that I attended (I spent two years at CBC and graduated from Nyack College after five years of schooling.) First, Columbia Bible College was a great school. It was listed as a Christian liberal arts school, but it had a devotional emphasis toward evangelism and missions. There were memorable chapels and great classes.

Columbia Bible College was founded on the traditions of the Keswick movement that flourished in England from the middle to the end of the 19th century and had a major effect on the spiritual life of America. It did not focus so much on correct Biblical doctrine for the inspiration of the believer, but on identifying with Christ, the repentance of sin, and a commitment to proclaiming the gospel, particularly in foreign lands. The emphasis was on attaining a higher spiritual life. Such pillars of our Christian faith as Donald Barnhouse, Hudson Taylor the great missionary to India, Andrew Murray, John Stott, and R.A. Torrey were its proponents and conference speakers. Alan Redpath, the pastor of the First Baptist Church in New York City and the acclaimed Stephen Olford spoke at our chapels and conferences. There were great books such as *The Blessed Hope* by George Eldon Ladd and *The Normal Christian Life* by Watchman Nee that were very inspirational at that time. This inspiration drove over eighty percent of CBC's alumni to the foreign mission fields. Although there was a lapse of a few years for me, Columbia's emphasis stayed with me throughout the years of my future ministry.

All students at Columbia had to participate in Christian service in our local community. In my first semester, I was assigned to be a chaplain at the orthopedic ward at the Veterans' Hospital in Columbia. Dealing with a longstanding fear of hospitals, I had to swallow hard as I went into the wards. However, I drew some comfort knowing that on the orthopedic ward most patients were going home soon. Unfortunately, this was not the case with one patient at the end of the hall, who lay in a bed surrounded by a curtain. I walked to the doorway and knocked before entering. There I found a man, twenty-nine years old, and his wife, and two small children. This young man who had dived into a swimming pool with shallow water had suffered a broken neck and was paralyzed from the neck down. What could I say? What could I do? The family was distraught. I read a few passages from Scripture and prayed as I did with all of the patients, but when I left this family with tears in my eyes, I prayed, "God, if you don't choose to give me the gift of healing, I don't think I can do this anymore, especially if it involves an assignment to a children's ward."

I had many other assignments, including preaching from a soapbox on a street corner while the Salvation Army band played hymns. There I learned to cope with the embarrassment of being heckled and how to handle the hecklers. I did counseling at the USO for servicemen, a stint with open-air campaigners preaching at bus stops and at construction sites with workers on their lunch break. Although these tasks were tough, they taught me two things. To be effective in your ministry, you have to be patient, and you must be very bold.

I grew a great deal through these experiences, and through CBC's academics I learned much Biblical truth, but I felt I still had a monkey on my back. Why had my church—the Roman Catholic Church—forsaken the founder of Christianity? They admitted that Jesus was God. Then why had His words and those of His apostles been abandoned, their authority as church teachings denied? What went wrong, I wondered. I was about to find out.

I want to state here that what follows in this and the next chapter is not a definitive defense of orthodox theology—I will leave that task to the giants of Reformation scholarship. The case I make here against both Roman Catholicism and Protestant Arminian dispensationalism is how, in my studies and experience, I learned the error of these false teachings. This is no way meant to be an exhaustive, thorough, or even scholarly examination of the two belief systems, but it is a witness to how I personally was set free from these theological inaccuracies. Also, I purposely did not structure my critique of these two subjects in topics or in an organized fashion. This because I wanted to approach these subjects as I encountered them, so please bear with me in the scramble of thoughts herein presented.

One of the first courses that I had at CBC was Church History. After studying early church history, our class began studies of the Middle Ages, and at that point, my professor gave us an assignment to write an eight-to-ten-page research paper on our studies thus far. Some of my classmates chose to write about great men like Ignatius, Origen, or Augustine. Others pursued subjects like the great councils and creeds of the church like the Apostle's Creed or the Nicene Creed used in the liturgy of many churches today. I, however, chose to research the authority of the Roman Catholic Church. I hoped that in this way I could finally remove the monkey from my back.

I loved the Roman Church—its majesty, reverence, and traditions. My mother and her family were staunch Roman Catholics going back many generations. But why had this strong church forsaken the teachings of Christ and the apostles as revealed in the Holy Scriptures? Why was this monkey on my back? Now I cannot produce my 2,500-word paper here (although I am sure it rests somewhere among the great literary works of our time) but I can summarize my findings.

I first decided to research the title pope, pontiff, or father because it was a somewhat authoritative name. I found out the name was first used in a letter by Dionysius the bishop of Alexandria around 248 AD, referring to Heraclas as our "blessed pope" or father. Surprisingly Dionysius meant the term "father" not for its authoritative meaning, but as an affectionate or endearing expression. However, as the bishops of Christian churches looked more and more to Rome for guidance, the bishops gave the title to that city's bishop, declaring that he had "Petrine Supremacy." If the bishops would have had any respect for the word of God, they would have stopped this practice immediately. "And call no man your father on the earth, for one is your Father, even He who is in heaven" (Matthew 23:9, ASV). The succeeding popes emphasized more the supremacy of the position than the fatherly aspect.

Around 1075, Pope Gregory VII issued the "*dictatus Papae*" that stated that the pope is the "universal" head over both the church and the state (F.C. Roberts, *To All Generations*, p. 87). Later, in the year 1138, Pope Innocent III declared the decretum—"papal omnipotence," power over everything in the universe including church, state, and the interpretation of Scripture. Thomas Aquinas, in his massive work *Summa Theologica* written between 1265-1273, put all of this into church theology, including papal infallibility. This policy was confirmed as recently as 1870 when during Vatican I it was decreed that when the pope spoke *ex cathedra* ("from the chair") concerning faith and morals, he spoke infallibly to the worldwide church.

So! Argument over. Who can argue with infallibility? Or with a person who claims to be infallible? He sets the rules (doctrine). This event changed Catholicism forever. Whatever proceeded from the Vatican would now be final for faith and practice for Catholics. This guaranteed the financial future of the church forever. For the Roman Catholic, this is, man trumps Scripture! Would I trust Jesus, the apostles, and inspired Scripture, or human agencies, councils, and traditions for truth? The monkey was off my back at last. I chose Christ directly.

I remember when I had my son, Billy, in a Little League game. He got on first base with a good hit. I was coaching third base, and the next player hit a long ball to left center. Billy ran to second, looked at me, and saw I was waving him to third. I knew it would be a close play. But this was a close game, and we were in the last inning, a couple of runs behind, and the bottom of the batting order would be coming up. The left fielder threw the ball, Billy slid. His hand touched the base just before the ball got there. I said, "Safe."

The umpire said, "Out!"

No matter how I argued, Billy was out! You can't argue an umpire's call on the field. It's in the rules. The commissioner set the rule; he's infallible in baseball.

I once argued with a Catholic friend who was very familiar with all of the issues. I made my best Scriptural case against extra-canonical teaching. He said I overlooked one thing—papal infallibility. If one accepts that premise, he must concede papal teaching regarding faith or morals is true! What other choice does he have? It is very frustrating. Trying to convince a person with that mindset is like trying to knock down a brick wall with a feather. At that point, I threw up my hands. I threw out some pertinent Scriptures—after all, God said His word will never come back empty but will accomplish what He intended, and is sharper than a two-edged sword (Isaiah 55:11; Hebrews 4:12).

My studies have shown me that the historic malady of man is his attempt to usurp power over God's authority. From Adam and Eve to all of the despots in history, including the pope. The egocentric heart seeks political and economic power over everything. This is what the Apostle John calls "the world" when he stated, "If anyone loves the world, love for the Father is not in him" (I John 2:15, AMP). The Apostle Paul adds, "For the love of money is the root of all kinds of evil" (I Timothy 6:10, ASV). Jesus said, "Ye cannot serve both God and money" (Matthew 6:24, NIV).

The doctrine of "papal omnipotence" (Innocent III, 1140 AD) was the climax of the early battle over the church and state in 1077 between Henry IV of the Holy Roman Empire and Pope Gregory VII. Gregory used his power to excommunicate Henry, the ultimate political and spiritual power. (F.C. Roberts, *To All Generations,* pp. 87-89).

I found that the doctrines of saint worship and purgatory also fit nicely into the principle of this world, namely power for economic gain. I believe that these doctrines were the foundation for the tremendous wealth of the Roman Church.

Purgatory, meaning a place of purging, is an intermediate place of suffering and pain where Catholics believe they will go to be "purified" of remaining sins (meaning they will pay for sins not yet forgiven). "Purified" or cleansing , really, is a disguise for earning or meriting your release from this dreadful place you are condemned to. Why else would the extra merits that Mary and the saints have accumulated be applied to those suffering through the prayers of relatives of those incarcerated there?

Merit means earning. Why has the Catholic Church rejected the Apostle Paul's claim, "There is therefore now **no condemnation** to them that are in Jesus Christ" (Romans 8:1a, KJV)? Is further condemnation needed?! Are Catholics not "in Christ"? Do they not have the Spirit?

The Roman church taught that there were three ways for you to get out of purgatory or at least have your time shortened there. First, you must suffer to earn merits until payment is made for your release. Secondly, and historically, your relatives can pay money to the Church to shorten your days there. The pope would issue a receipt in the form of an indulgence to the payee. This practice was ended after the Protestant Reformation. Thirdly, your relatives can pray to the saints, asking for some of their extra merit above what they needed for their own salvation which are stored in a "bank of merit" to be applied to your account by Mary and other saints. Now you have two options—suffering to earn merits or pray to the saints for them to have mercy upon you. I thanked God that I was justified by faith and had "peace with God through our Lord Jesus Christ." (Romans 5:1, KJV). I realized at the end of my paper that my mother and her family labored under the delusion that they could earn their way to ultimate salvation. No Roman Catholic can have ultimate peace. For me, my salvation was a free gift given to me by God with faith that I exercised to the satisfaction of my Heavenly Father. I had true peace! (Ephesians 2:8-9).

This corrupt and misguided system goes on even to this day. It has raised billions and billions for the Roman Catholic Church; further, this system has created a fearful psychological and physical dependence of Catholics on the Roman church and not on Christ alone for ultimate salvation. The outcome of saint worship has led to religious mechanicalism among Catholics, a practice that our Lord bitterly opposed in the Pharisees—routine, repetitive, legalistic acts with no real spiritual heartfelt meaning. ("And in praying, use not vain repetitions, as the Gentiles do: (for example, the rosary) for they think that they shall be heard for their much speaking" (Matthew 6:7, ASV).

I discovered that beyond vain repetitions, Jesus reminds us that the deeper problem is hypocrisy. This is prevalent for Roman Catholics (found in other denominations also, but particularly in the Roman system) in the form of "routinism" and traditionalism where churchgoers think they are doing good and righteous acts but are committing the most grievous sin of all—hypocrisy. These people start out with sincerity, but for many, it leads to an outward practice of religion with no humble, deep spiritual meaning. This was the plight of the Pharisee coming to pray (Luke 18:9-11). He regularly and with great routine became very self-confident in accomplishing the laws (rules) laid down by his religious system. Now I am not saying all Roman Catholics are like this Pharisee, however many come to worship routinely with the self-confidence that they are following the traditions expected of them by the religious system, when actually they miss the entire point, namely begging for mercy because of they are sinners. This is exactly what the lowly tax collector did, and he went out justified.

Some years ago I had a close friend, Douglas Culver, now deceased, who was a scholar with multiple PhDs after his name. He was also a great orator, as well as President of the President's Council on Religion and Economics. His prayers were humble and eloquent, and he always ended them with "Thank you God for sins forgiven." How important mercy is. Jesus actually came to set us free from a system of traditionalism and routinism. It is Christmastime now when I am writing this book, a time God has, because of His Son, declared peace with mankind. No Roman Catholic has real peace. Purgatory always crouches at his door. There is no peace even for the monastic who has buried his talent (ability), avoiding any return for his Master (Matthew 25:14-30).

I have learned that systems with these requirements, routines, and traditions tend to make people dependent on the system rather on God alone.

A second and more devastating teaching of the Roman Catholic Church was their practice of intentionally withholding the divinely inspired words of Scripture from the masses. They blame this corrupt policy on God Himself.

> *That it has pleased God to make Holy Scripture obscure in certain places lest, if it were perfectly clear to all, it might be vulgarized and subjected to disrespect or be so misunderstood by people of limited intelligence as to lead them into error. —Gregory VII (Ephraim Emerton, The Correspondence of Pope Gregory VII: Selected Letters from the Registrum)*

Gregory, how convenient! The obvious question is, why in an age of eighty percent world literacy, has the church not reversed this teaching of Gregory's? After all, almost everyone can read even the newspaper! The answer is quite obvious. The church did not want to jeopardize its extra-biblical teachings and possibly lose the tremendous income that these doctrines produce. The house of cards would come tumbling down. For me, my conclusion was that the church robbed the masses of God's word for financial gain. If the church leaders had opened the Bible to the people, they could have read, "There is therefore now no condemnation to them that are in Christ Jesus" (Romans 8:1, ASV). "And having made peace through the blood of his cross, by him to reconcile all things unto himself (Colossians 1:20, KJV)."

Exposure of the people to the Bible and particularly the New Testament would have dealt a serious blow to the church's nest egg. The people, however, would have had the truth.

Luther's principle remains true: "The Bible is sufficiently clear in content to yield its meaning to the believer." He added, "The Bible became the property of all Christians," (*Protestant Biblical Interpretation*, Bernard Ramm, p. 55). The question remains, how can we be justified (have right standing with God) and not be justified at the same time? How can we have peace with God (Romans 5:1) and suffer at His hands at the same time? It's either believe God in His Word or believe human agency. It's that simple.

The Catholic system also seemed to create a dichotomy regarding Christian living. The New Testament reminds us that as a true Christian, I have Christ within me; I take Him along on all of the activities of the day—business, sports, family ("whatsoever ye do, do all to the glory of God," I Corinthians 10:31, KJV; also, "that in all things He might have the preeminence," Colossians 1:18, ASV). If I sin, I take care of it with confession and repentance as soon as I am aware of it (I John 1:9). When I was a Catholic, I would tell myself that when sins accumulated that I would go over to the church by and by and have the priest take care of them. It's as if I could trash my car, cramming it for a couple of weeks and when it was finally ready to break down, taking it to the garage and having a mechanic fix it. Now I know that the Roman Catholic Church doesn't want its members to think that way, but in reality, that is the way it is for most Catholics. One way was living for Christ, in Christ, and with Christ every day. The other was a false hope in a weekend fix.

One final doctrine that clinched my exit from Catholicism was the church's teaching on grace. Thomas Aquinas in his book *Summa Theologica* taught that at death unrepentant people go right to Hades. Repentant people receive "free grace" so that they can pursue "good works" to "earn merits" toward final salvation (F.C. Roberts, *To All Generations*, pp. 119-129).

The Apostle Paul, on the other hand, wrote, "Being justified freely by His grace" (Romans 3:24, ASV). His word also says, "for by grace have ye been saved through faith; and that not of yourselves, it is the gift of God; *not of works*" (Ephesians 2:8-9, ASV, emphasis mine). I guess the question came down to who's infallible—the human pope, often corrupt (Peter DeRosa, *Vicars of Christ: The Dark Side of the Papacy*), or the ever loving, freely forgiving, all-righteous God?

This is the conclusion that my studies have thus far shown me. I say I am sorry to my Roman Catholic friends. I know most are sincere, humble, and believing people. I thank God that Jesus said, "Him that cometh to me I will in no wise cast out" (John 6:37, ASV) and the Scriptures say God looks on the heart, not the outward appearances. I encourage all to read the infallible word of God in the Holy Scripture. There they will find the true meaning of grace that leads to right standing with God and ultimate peace.

In addition, my study gave me a new appreciation for the reformers of the Reformation. Not only did they stand for the principles of the gospel, they also stood against the prince of this world whose ultimate weapon is the lust for power, prestige, and money.

I might add that I only got a B- on that paper. My professor told me that although my content was good, I tried to cover too broad a scope.

Although my college experience was rich and full, I had not forgotten about my desire to pursue a pilot's license. Every dollar that I had after paying for essentials like snacks and gas was spent on flying lessons taken in the cheapest possible airplane—a J-3 Cub at Columbia County Airport. When I left CBC,

I had a long way to go to earn a private ticket, but I was on my way to becoming a pilot.

Wonderful the matchless grace of Jesus…
Purchasing peace and heaven,
For all eternity
Wonderful the matchless grace of Jesus,
Deeper than the mighty rolling sea
Higher than the mountain,
sparkling like a fountain,
All-sufficient grace for even me!
Broader than the scope of my transgressions,
Greater far than all my sin and shame;
Oh, magnify the precious Name of Jesus,
Praise His Name!

— Haldor Lillenas (based on Ephesians 1:8)

CHAPTER VII

EVERY WIND OF DOCTRINE

Till we all attain unto the unity of faith, and of the knowledge of the Son of God, unto a full-grown man, unto the measure of the stature of the fulness of Christ: that we may be no longer children, tossed to and fro and carried about with every wind of doctrine, by the sleight of men (Ephesians 4:13-14, ASV).

I had a girlfriend when I was at Columbia; her name was Betty Russell, and she was very beautiful. She was a true Southern belle and had a deep Southern accent.

The college was very legalistic and had strict rules for couples—no physical contact at any time, including no holding hands, or giving a hug goodbye. An allowed date was meeting her in the lobby of the girls' dorm at six, walking together and sitting with her at dinner. Then walking her back to the dorm by seven. That's it. Well, this policy was destined to clash with this individualistic ex-Marine.

One Thursday at dinner, Betty told me that she was going home for the weekend. She lived in Sumter, South Carolina, and it just happened that I had a Christian service assignment at a fairground just a few miles from Sumter that Saturday night. I thought to myself, "This is great. I'll just stop by her house on my way back to college." So I did. We went out for a barbeque and a root beer at the local Piggy Park and I dropped her off back home. This, however, made me late for curfew and all of the doors of my dorm were locked. So I climbed up to the roof, went to a spot just above my room. I reached over and knocked on my window. My roommate opened the window and helped me swing into the room. Safe! I didn't even have to sign in and explain why I was late. Monday morning I ate breakfast and went to two classes. Then while I was going to our daily ten o'clock chapel, a fellow student came to me and said, "Mr. Braswell wants to see you in his office right away."

Now Braswell was Dean of Students, a large, gruff man who was unpopular with most students. This did not bode well. As I sat across from the dean's desk, he began the inquisition. "Someone," he said, "reported to me that your car was seen in Sumter Saturday night."

Caught. I had violated my own standards: Obey the rules that you committed to keep, even if you don't agree with them. I deserved whatever punishment I was to receive. What could I say? Ask for mercy? Give an excuse? I had learned as a Marine, Marines don't ever ask for mercy and never give excuses. Excuses only increase the penalty. Braswell repeated, "Was your car seen in Sumter on Saturday night?"

"Yes, sir."

"Did you see Ms. Russell?"

"Yes, sir."

"Did you have any physical contact with Ms. Russell?"

(I wanted to say, "I need a lawyer.") "Yes, sir."

"Did you have more physical contact with Ms. Russell than a kiss?"

"No, sir."

He dropped his pencil on his desk and said, "You have one hour to pack your bags and be off campus."

Kicked out! The penalty was harsh. I lost all academic credit for that almost completed semester, and all the money paid for the semester, and now out on my own. However, I understood well. If Braswell had given me a second chance it would have sent a very bad message to the rest of the student body—the rules are just a joke, like a dog barking with no bite. If there are not severe consequences for breaking the rules, why do you need to be held accountable at all? The reasons for accountability then would be fallacious.

Despite that incident, I had a great experience at Columbia; I had Mr. Hatch, a man I greatly respected and I loved that course. I learned that my salvation produced repentance initiated by the grace of God through faith alone, not by my effort, or my earning of merits. The music and hymns sung and the chapel speakers inspire me to this day. I learned that my right standing before God does not depend upon my merit or effort. I lost my fear of hecklers, embarrassment, and hospitals, and I learned to be proud to carry the gospel in ministry. I learned from CBC and the obstacle course that there's no easy way. You have to run hard with endurance, practice continually, keep the rules, and know every angle as you approach difficulties in life and ministry.

While I was at Columbia, my father sold the farm. He also sold Spanjer Brothers to the Chicago office, and he moved to Florida. He bought a forty-acre farm outside of Ocala, got a herd of purebred polled Charolais beef cattle, moved Olga, Rodger and Chrissy (who had been born to Dad and Olga after I returned from Germany) to the new farm and retired.

Meanwhile, I headed north—back to my home church and good friends. I got a job with Leonard Roe who ran a logging business. He paid me two dollars an hour plus room and board. My room was in an unfinished basement, and my food was his wife Juanita's Mexican cuisine—rice and beans. Logging was backbreaking work; Homelite did not make lightweight chainsaws in those days, and I had to operate one eight to ten hours a day. But those were good days. I made less than a hundred dollars a week and spent it all on flying lessons. I worked for Leonard from that winter through the following fall. I was ready to go back to school.

Example of work Bill did for Leonard;
A giant walnut log would be sold for making walnut veneer.

I applied to Nyack College and was accepted to start that spring semester. Twenty-five miles north of Manhattan, Nyack is a Christian liberal arts college, and it was great! Although it is a denominational school with the Christian and Missionary Alliance church, it had excellent professors in the theology department, particularly Doctors Cannon, Kenyon, and Kramer.

Now that I had become a Protestant Christian, I wanted to know more about the Protestant churches to discover one which I wanted to be part of. Along this line, one of my professors created an analogy comparing the various denominations to a candy store. He related that when you go into the Protestant "candy store" there are numerous selections. There are the mainline churches that have given up on the gospel. Churches like the United Presbyterian, most Anglican (Episcopalian in the U.S.), and most Methodist churches, these are like fireballs that burn all the way down. Don't buy into them at all. There are fundamentalist churches that are like jawbreakers—very legalistic and hard to swallow. Baptists are like almond Hershey bars—very sweet and pleasant to the taste, but the almonds (adult baptism only) are spiritually hard to digest. Independent Bible churches are like M&Ms. They come in many colors and varieties but have a hard shell of legalism and exclusiveness. He went on. There are Pentecostal churches that are like cotton candy—when you bite down, there is no content there. Finally, he said, there are Reformed churches that are like a bag of a variety of sweet chocolates—good content.

We all had a good laugh, but then our professor got serious. Continuing with a different analogy, he said that all of these denominations except the mainline group (which deny the gospel) and the Reformed churches, which make up about eighty percent of evangelical Christian churches are infected with a very serious foreign disease. This ailment is not fatal if caught early, although he warned, some have succumbed to it. Its effects are mostly blindness and the inability of those infected to know ultimate truth. Well, we wanted to know, what is this epidemic? He did not want to tell us. "Close the door," he told us. "It is Arminian dispensationalism."

"What is that? And what is the remedy?" one student asked.

"Well, what it is will be our course of study for the next three months," the professor stated. "The remedy is, for those infected, twenty ccs daily of Reformation theology." Understandably, we all wanted to know more. So our study began. I will try to condense it here. To understand this "malady," we have to look across the pond. The old saying is true "As goes Europe, so goes the United States." Bernie Sanders would have been run out of town in the 1950s, '60s, and '70s with his progressive socialism. But it became popular in Europe, and now Bernie runs for president and draws millions of votes!

A similar thing happened with theological liberalism in the late 1800s and early 1900s. It appeared first in the form of modernism, originating in the works of Friedrich Schleiermacher's *On Religion* and Immanuel Kant's *Religion Within the Limits of Reason Alone* (New Dictionary of Theology, IVP).

The logic and reasoning of these men are very academic, complicated and, I thought, hard to follow and consequently, I didn't do well in my philosophy of religion classes. I passed the course with a C+. However, I understood well the outcome and effects of their respective philosophies. Schleiermacher's teaching that experience is the basis of knowing truth and Kant's reason as the basis for truth, ruled out all supernatural intervention by God in history, and the view of the Bible as being inspired revelation. It was a human book, relegated to legend and fable at best to teach children. They also taught that Jesus, although He was a moral teacher, was not divine; they acknowledged the historical Jesus was a good and moral person only. Of course, they did away with the incarnation, substitutionary atonement, and resurrection. This all was verified by Kant's view of Scripture. "The Scripture will be seen as a descriptive record of human religious experience but as having no authority beyond that" (New Dictionary of Theology, p. 363).

Immanuel Kant claimed that all religions lead to God. They denied that man is sinful by nature and that he is progressing higher and higher to moral and ethical perfection. In fact, they believed that this universal moral progress of man will eventually usher in the Kingdom of God. This philosophy of theology tore the guts out of the gospel, and the effects of this theology remain to this day. Moreover, the spread of these teachings throughout Europe gave theological schools in universities a big break. Religious thinkers could be no longer embarrassed, they could join the "Science and Reason" club and be at peace with the secular university community.

In a half-hearted effort to regain Reformation theology, theologians in Europe such as Karl Barth, Brunner, and Bultmann sought to make Christianity more relevant. But as usual for that age, they attacked Scripture as a human, fallible, and an errant document. These gave birth to "neo-orthodoxy," a new truth in understanding theology. But it was the old "truth" wrapped in a new package called modernism or liberalism.

This new teaching came to America like a tidal wave; it came in the form of experientialism (Schleiermacher's teaching that true religion is an individual experience) and Bultmann's neo-orthodoxy (the "new" truth about religion). This theological philosophy hit our major universities' divinity schools—Harvard, Yale, and Princeton—like feeding starving people peanut-butter-and-jelly sandwiches. They gobbled it up! These schools sent out hundreds of newly ordained clergy to replace pastors who were retiring from mainline churches (Anglican, Presbyterian, Methodist, and others) all over the eastern United States. Original sin is contrary to "enlightened" scholarship and is learned behavior. You can overcome your tendency to do bad or evil by discipline and following the example of Jesus. The preceding are historical facts and do not need formal documentation.

Well, this teaching didn't go over well in the Bible belt of the South. Neither did it go over well with fundamental or Pentecostal churches and particularly the congregations of Bible-thumping Baptists. They clung to their inspired Bibles with a death grip. The problem was that these denominations really had no systematic theology to support their enthusiastic belief in the Bible. No problem! Here comes a hero riding a white horse from England to save the day. It was like the old radio show "The Lone Ranger and Tonto," aka John Darby and C.I. Scofield. Their white horse was called "Arminian Dispensationalism" (hereafter in this book referred to as A.D.F.T.—Arminian Dispensationalism False Teaching).

Darby and Scofield came out of a small Plymouth Brethren sect in England. They authored a major false teaching on the evangelical church in the United States. However, their claim that the Bible was literally true and inerrant was just what Baptist Fundamentals and Pentecostals wanted to hear. They embraced it lock, stock, and barrel (William E. Cox, *An Examination of Dispensationalism*, p. 11). But C.I. Scofield said that the Bible must be interpreted by one system. This system would deny the sovereignty of God. They denied that God was sovereign in the initiation of individual salvation; they denied that God could initiate His intervention in history unless asked for and approved by man. The popular motto of A.D.F.T. was that "God proposes, man disposes." Or as S.D. Gordon put it in *Quiet Talks about Jesus*, "Everything must be done with man's consent," (William E. Cox, *An Examination of Dispensationalism*, p. 31). Further, A.D.F.T. denies the covenant of grace that God proclaims throughout Scriptures.

I was amazed and still am that grace, the free gift to man by God through Christ has brought such controversy. One side says it's not effective unless you earn it, the other says it's not effective unless you ask for it. Both put salvation in the hands of man, not God. They both want to strip God of His sovereignty and exert human control over the activities of God. Do we believe the words of Paul to the Ephesians when he said that this grace and faith is "not of your own"? You cannot pay for it nor intellectually earn it. If you could, it would not be a gift! (Ephesians 2:8-9, Romans 9:16, II Timothy 1:9).

A.D.F.T. divides Biblical history into seven dispensations (ages); grace only applies to the church age according to A.D.F.T.'s teaching (William E. Cox, *An Examination of Dispensationalism*, pp. 17-18, quoting Lewis Sperry Chafer, *Dispensationalism*). In other dispensations, man has right standing with God by "legal obedience" to the laws of God (ibid).

Finally, for me anyway, the most grievous insult of A.D.F.T. is the claim that Rome had the right to crucify our Lord. A.D.F.T. teaches that Christ offered an earthly kingdom to the Jews. They sent Him to Pilate accused of insurrection (William E. Cox, *An Examination of Dispensationalism*, p. 31, referring to W.E. Blackstone, *Jesus is Coming,* and M.R. DeHaan, *Second Coming of Jesus*).

If this accusation were true, Pilate would have been justified in condemning Jesus. Any claim to overthrow Caesar would have demanded the death penalty. After lengthy questioning of Jesus, however, Pilate said three times, I find no fault in this man (Luke 23:4, 14, 22). In fact, he called Jesus a "righteous man" (Matthew 27:24, ASV). Pilate then gave into the Jews and had Jesus crucified—a totally unjustified crucifixion.

Another false teaching of A.D.F.T. is the distinction it makes between Israel and the church. The Apostle Paul teaches that there is no distinction between the Jew (Israel) and the Greek (Gentile). Now, according to St. Paul they are one "new man" into "one body unto God," (Ephesians 2:14-16). In fact, the Apostle even uses the New Testament term church (*ekklesia*) applied to Moses in the Old Testament—"This is He (Christ) that was in the church in the wilderness" (Acts 7:38) (Ecclesia, *Expository Dictionary of the New Testament Words,* W.E. Vines, p. 83).

John Bright, in his great book *The Kingdom of God*, states, "The Church is the true Israel of God" (Galatians 6:16), "a remnant according to the election of grace," (Romans 11:5), "And if ye are Christ's, then are ye Abraham's seed, heirs according to the promises," (Galatians 3:29)" (*The Kingdom of God*, p. 227). I became convinced that contrary to A.D.T.F., Christ is the unifying factor of all Scripture.

Another false teaching of dispensationalism is its doctrine of the pre-millennial return of Jesus Christ. This belief is found nowhere in Scripture unless you misinterpret Revelation 20:6, that Christ "shall reign with Him a thousand years" (ASV). Now we know that a thousand years in apocalyptic (symbolic) books means a long period of time. And we know that Christ's kingdom came after His atonement on the cross. We know this because Jesus said previously "I shall not eat it until it be fulfilled in the kingdom of God" (Luke 22:16-18, ASV). The atonement then took place. The disciples were assembled, and Jesus said, "Have ye here anything to eat... He took it and ate before them" (Luke 24:40, 43, ASV). The kingdom of God was not at hand any longer—it had come! The announcement was clear. His coronation would take place at Pentecost when He was seated at the right hand of the Father (Ephesians 1:20-22). The millennium-long period had begun. The strong man was now bound. The gospel could go forth. We might ask, as the disciples did, "What shall be the sign of thy coming and of the end of the world?" (Matthew 24:3, ASV) "And the gospel of the kingdom shall be preached in the whole world for a testimony unto all the nations; and then shall the end come" (Matthew 24:14, ASV).

The Apostle Paul give us a clear timeline of the end times in 1 Corinthians 15:23-24. "Each in his own order: Christ the first-fruits; then they that are Christ's at his coming. Then cometh the end, when he shall deliver up the kingdom to God"

(ASV). Bernard Ramm in his great little book, *Protestant Biblical Interpretation,* reminds us that we must always go to the clearest texts to define doctrine. A.D.F.T. does not practice that hermeneutical principle. There are many passages that make it clear that at Christ's return, final judgment, and the end of the age occurs. Do the followers of A.D.F.T. really believe that Christ would return to earth for a thousand years to be spit upon and rejected by man a second time? Please run away from that teaching as I did in 1964.

Proof texts that at Jesus Christ's second coming (*parousia* = appearing) the "end of the age," resurrection of the dead and final judgment occur:

The end of the age and judgment at His appearing—Matthew 13:39-40, 47-50; 22:1-14; 25:14-30

Apostle Paul links final judgment and resurrection of dead at Christ's appearing—2 Thessalonians 1:6-9

Last days at the same time as judgment—John 12:48

Final judgment and resurrection of dead are one event at the second coming—Revelations 20:11-15

Conclusion: Jesus, John, and Paul connect final judgment, the end of the age, and the resurrection of the dead to Jesus's second coming. No place for a continuing thousand-year reign of Christ and future earthly activity.

A.D.F.T. makes finding out truth in Scripture very complicated. Martin Luther also had insight into this problem when he talked about the sufficiency principle of interpreting Scripture. He claimed that the Scriptures are sufficiently clear enough for the common man to understand. This is also known as perspicuity, or clearness, of Scripture. I cannot understand why A.D.F.T. falsely makes the understanding of Biblical truth so complicated that you have to have two PhDs after your name to figure it out.

After this study and others, I was determined that I would

never settle in any A.D.F.T. church. As for me, I chose the grace theme of interpreting Scripture, set out by the great Reformation thinkers like Martin Luther, John Calvin, John Knox, Charles Spurgeon, George Whitefield, Jonathan Edwards as well as theological leaders of today such as J.I. Packer, R.C. Sproul, D. James Kennedy, Albert Mohler, John MacArthur, and numerous others who believe the Bible is the story of God's grace to mankind. Grace and mercy was bestowed on those who did not ask for it, like Adam and Eve when God clothed them, like Seth, Noah, and Abraham, like Isaac, Jacob, Joseph, and Moses, Joshua, the judges, and Samuel, King David, and the prophets, Ezra, Nehemiah, Esther, and the apostles—none ever asked for grace or mercy. God gave it to them and caused them to believe in His promises, that one day a savior would come and be their king. He would provide redemption. This king, by His sovereign grace and mercy, would save His people from the consequences of their sin. I believe the theme of the Bible is: I will be your God, and you will be My people (Genesis 17:7, Exodus 6:7, Leviticus 26:12, Jeremiah 31:33, 2 Corinthians 6:16, Titus 2:14 and Revelation 21:3). These people will come into His Kingdom by God's pure grace and by faith alone.

God did not say, "I will be your God if you pay Me or earn My favor." He did not say, "I will be your God if you ask and beg Me to be your God." He said, "I will be your God, and you will be My people." A sovereign decree planned before the foundations of the universe were laid. No human agency can put conditions on this declaration.

I had come to believe that the covenant of grace provides the unity and continuity that binds all Scripture together. It is simple in purpose and understandable in content so that even a simple, dyslexic former Marine like me can get it.

In summary, during the Renaissance, European unbelief

in the gospel came steamrolling into America on the backs of modernism and neo-orthodoxy. It eventually would destroy the truth of the gospel in great denominations, such as the United Presbyterian Church and the Methodism of John and Charles Wesley, making these denominations mere religious social groups. It destroyed the faith of an entire generation. The remaining evangelical churches (Baptists, Fundamentalists, Pentecostals and others) tried to fight off this onslaught, but it came on them like a wolf in sheep's clothing and a real Trojan horse. This attack did not break the evangelical spirit. Although the false teaching of Arminian Dispensationalism sought to stem the tide, it ultimately failed. I live in the generation that is restoring the gospel back into Christianity and giving it solid Scriptural foundations. This movement is known as the rebirth of the Reformation movement, led by such great theologians as Packer, Sproul, and many others. They speak of the grace of Christ for the complete forgiveness of sin, offered by faith alone, freely to those that believe, by a sovereign God—Jesus Christ Himself—to rescue His elect (Titus 1:1, Mark 13:20, Revelation 17:14, Luke 18:7).

My exit from Catholicism and Arminian Dispensationalism started me on a long academic journey towards discipleship. From that experience, I learned two important truths. First, that ultimate truth—moral, ethical, redemptive or otherwise—can only be found in the Word of God. Secondly, that studying it in its entirety and with prayer, its meaning was clear enough that even an dyslexic country boy like me could learn its essential truths.

I had a vivid lesson taught to me earlier by my experience with Bob Hoppe when at sea in 1957. Upon his dramatic conversion, he had only a little New Testament that transformed his life, in spite of strong Catholic opposition. He and I had no theologians, Biblical scholars, expositors. We were only simple Marines being confronted and guided by the Word of God alone. The complexities of scholarship and division would come but for me, *sola Scriptura* was enough.

During the summer of '65, between my junior and senior years at Nyack, I worked for Don Castner in his moving business. I was provided with a truck and two helpers. It was another backbreaking job—moving refrigerators and hide-a-beds up five-floor walk-ups in the Bronx was a killer. Once we had to move an evicted family from their home. Excavators and bull-dozers were standing by, waiting to demolish the home as soon as we were done. The police were there also. As we approached the home, I wondered why they were going to destroy this poor family's home. I soon found out why. Feces was squished on mattresses where someone had rolled over on them. Pails in corners were filled with poop and urine. The refrigerator was filled with rotten food covered in cat hair. Although we were to take everything out and pile it in the yard, I couldn't take it any-more. I threw up and went and sat in my truck.

All in all the moving experience paid off. I learned how to move prize furniture safely with no nicks and scratches. People often gave big tips for the care we gave, and I made almost two thousand dollars in tips alone that summer, and I spent it all on flying lessons.

> "Thy word is a lamp unto my feet and a light unto my path... The entrance of thy words giveth light; it giveth understanding unto the simple"
> —Psalm 119:105,130, KJV

CHAPTER VIII

THE AVIATION DEVIATION, PART I
THE "CHAMP"

Oh! I have slipped the surly bonds of Earth
And danced the skies on laughter-silvered wings;
Sunward I've climbed, and joined the tumbling mirth
Of sun-split clouds, and done a hundred things
You have not dreamed of—wheeled and soared
and swung
High in the sunlit silence. Hov'ring there,
I've chased the shouting wind along, and flung
My eager craft through footless halls of air

Up, up the long, delirious burning blue
I've topped the wind-swept heights with easy grace
Where never lark, or ever eagle flew—
And, while with silent lifting mind I've trod
The high untrespassed sanctity of space,
Put out my hand, and touched the face of God.
—High Flight, John Gillespie Magee, Jr.

In 1964 I was ready to take my first solo flight. It went like this. I had flown the cheapest airplanes I could rent, either a Piper Cub or an Aeronca Champion (Champ). Both had tandem seating—student in front and instructor in back. The Champ, with which I was most familiar, was a tailwheel airplane that was prop starting. (You had to spin the propeller to start it, taking two people—one seated inside with his feet on the brakes and the other "propping" the propeller.) It had a sixty-horsepower continental engine. Russ, my flight instructor at that time, said he wanted to upgrade to the Piper Tri-Pacer. When I asked him why, he said, "If you're going to solo, you need to learn in a more sophisticated airplane."

The Tri-Pacer had a more powerful 125-horsepower engine. It also had radio navigation, and it was steered on the ground with a nose wheel. It was, however, ten dollars more an hour to rent.

Now Russ weighed over three hundred pounds, and I always thought the change in planes was because Russ knew we would be over the weight limit in the Champ. Anyway, I became familiar with the Tri-Pacer flying in the pattern. The pattern consists of a rectangle over the airport. If the airfield is at four hundred feet above sea level, you must enter the downwind leg at 1400 feet, or 1000 feet above the field.

Let me explain the pattern. I would start at one end of the runway. After a quick preflight check, I would put the throttle to full power, and the stick full forward until the tail would come up. At about sixty-five miles per hour in a Champ, I gave slight backpressure to the stick, and the plane lifted off nicely. Next, I took the head off the power (that is, drop it to about 2,300 rpm) and would fly straight ahead until I was about 500 feet above the field (900 feet on the altimeter.) At that checkpoint, I was over a particular farm, and then I'd make a ninety-degree left turn and keep climbing. This was the crosswind leg of the pattern. When I reached 1400 feet on the altimeter, 1000 feet above the Sussex airfield, I was passing over a small lake. At that point, I made another ninety-degree left turn onto the downwind leg, which runs parallel to the runway. I'd pulled the power back to cruising speed, and I'd have one minute to relax. While the plane was flying parallel to the end of the runway, I'd pull the carburetor heat on and power back to about 1,500 rpm. I'd keep the nose level and go into a power glide. The plane descended to about 900 feet over Route 23 when I'd make a second ninety-degree turn, and enter the base leg. As I crossed over the village of Sussex, I'd make a final ninety-degree left turn onto the final approach to the runway. Keeping the plane lined up with the centerline of the runway I descended to the field, adding power if I was a little low, taking power off if I was high. When I was a few feet over the end of the runway, the "hole" as it is called, I would take off power and glide to a proper landing.

After flying the pattern four or five times on a Saturday morning, Russ said, "I'm going to let you try it by yourself." Wow! No instructor with me! Now with Russ in the narrow cabin in this Tri-Pacer, I was squished, hardly able to operate the controls. When he got out of the plane, I felt free! I had room. The only problem was the airplane felt free as well, over 300 pounds lighter! I was at an altitude of 1,000 feet over the farm and then more than 2,000 over the pond. On the downwind leg, not only was I 1,000 feet above the pattern (a danger to other planes crossing the airfield) but the field looked like a postage stamp. No one had warned me about this problem. How would I get down? My checkpoints were meaningless at this point. So I extended my downwind leg beyond the village and made two ninety-degree turns. The runway was so far away that I could hardly see it. To make matters worse, I was coming in too low. I could have landed on Main Street in the village of Sussex. I added power and eventually made a reasonable landing—I had soloed! When I taxied up, I saw that Russ was sweating profusely, but he let me do a few more landings to make the adjustments. I was a pilot! It was a dream come true.

The next step was securing my private pilot's license, which I accomplished that fall. Now I wanted a commercial pilot's license so that I could get paid to do what I loved doing. At that time, however, a candidate for a commercial pilot's license had to accumulate 200 hours before submitting an application. At $25 per hour to rent an airplane, those hours would cost me almost $4,000. So I went back to Paul Stieger at Sussex Airport where I had learned to fly, and asked, "Hey, Paul, would you sell me that Aeronca Champ I rented from you?" Now that plane was forty years old at that time.

Paul was a man of few words, and he replied, "$1500."

I said, "Can I pay you installments? $500, $500, and $500?"

"Yeah," he said.

But there was one problem! I didn't have $1500. I went to Paul and asked if he could wait until the end of the month. "Yeah," he said, "but no more than thirty days."

Ugh, the pressure was on. I figured that I would try to get the money in one of two ways. First, I had been offered a second part-time job at Paone's Pizza Parlor in Nyack. It was a dirty job—cleaning floors and ovens, washing pots and pans late at night after Sal Paone closed. I knew this job would take time away from my studies, but I took it anyway. The second idea I had was to try to form a flying club at the college. I would charge each member $100 to join, and they would pay $5 per flight hour, the money going to maintenance, and then they would top off the gas after use. The first part-time job I had was as a school bus driver for the Rockland Coach Lines. So I went to O'Neill, the manager and said, "Can you give me another run? I need the money."

"Sure," he answered, "if you want to take kids every Saturday to New York City." Well, I didn't want to drive a forty-four-passenger school bus filled with forty screaming Jewish kids in and out of the city with—here's the kicker—no chaperone! But it paid $30 a trip—two trips every Saturday. That was $60 a day with four Saturdays left, for a total of $240. That plus Paone's at

$5 an hour at three hours a night, six days a week for four weeks would net another $300. Adding the bus run and Paone's would get me to $760. Then, if I could add eight club members at $100 apiece, I would be home free. We would own a plane. A lot of things would have to come together, but I had a plan!

The first charter to New York City was on a Saturday afternoon. The bus was crammed with about fifty kids, and I was off, but I had no idea where I was going. O'Neill's directions were, "Just get into the Bronx, and the kids will tell you where the stops are."

The kids? The oldest one was ten! Well, I sat him right behind me, and we took off with kids screaming, yelling, throwing things out of the windows. Within minutes my head was pounding, and I thought, "What did I get myself into?" We headed down the Major Deegan, got off at Willis Avenue to the Cross Bronx Expressway, and on to the Grand Concourse. I was in the heart of the Bronx. "Now, little Isaac, you take over—that is if I can hear you."

"Pull over at the next light," I looked ahead and saw a group of parents waiting. Ten kids off. I continued on. Suddenly Isaac said, "I'm getting a little confused."

"Oh, great," I thought.

"Wait, turn here quick! Turn right here!" So I did, onto a wide street. Strange though. There was no traffic. I proceeded to go about three bus lengths down the street when up ahead a light must have changed because all of a sudden there were about twenty cars coming at me, head on. I realized with a shock that I was on a one-way street, going the wrong way. Before I knew it horns were blowing, people were screaming, cops were coming with red and yellow lights flashing. I was in a mess! Fortunately, the police officer solved the problem. "I'll watch you," he said, "but you'll have to back up to the Concourse. When you get there, pull over—I'll have to give you two tickets. One for going the wrong way down a one-way street, and the other for backing a school bus in the city limits."

"But you told me to back up, sir," I said.

"Did you back up or not?" he asked. "It doesn't matter who told you. You backed up. You can't back up a school bus within the city limits. It's the law." What could I say?

I got the rest of the kids home safely. When I got back to Nyack, I thought, "Thank God that nightmare is over." But it wasn't—not yet.

I told O'Neill about the trip and asked him if I could get the company to pay the tickets. "No, sir," he said. "Tickets are your responsibility. You need to watch what you are doing."

I pleaded with him but to no avail. This was going to take a bite out of my Aeronca Champ fund. The next Saturday evening found me in the Bronx traffic night court. "All pleading guilty to my left," the officer in charge stated. "All pleading guilty with an excuse to my right." Well, I thought, I had a good excuse. The kids told me to turn onto the one-way street, and the police officer told me to back up! So I went to the right. The judge started with the guilty pleas. "Jones, how do you plead?"

"Guilty, your honor." was the reply.

"Fifty dollars. Pay the clerk."

And so it went with all those who pled guilty. Then it got to those of us with excuses. The clerk looked at his clipboard and called, "Alphonso speeding on the Concourse." Then to the man in question, "What is your excuse?"

"I had to rush home, Your Honor. My mother-in-law was having a baby, sir."

The judge said quickly. "$200. Pay the clerk," said the judge. And so it went. Those with excuses had a double fine. I got the message.

When it came to me, I said, "Guilty, sir."

He said, "$100. Pay the clerk." I had learned an important lesson, but it threw me $100 short on my agreement with Paul.

The following Sunday my thirty days would be up. I had $700 from my two part-time jobs, six college students had paid to get into the flying club—that was $1360, but I lost $100 in court. I was $240 short. I put the $1360 into an envelope and headed to Sussex.

I explained my situation to Paul. "Paul," I said, "I have two other students joining the club, but their money has not come in yet. Can you give me another week?"

"One week, that's it," he stated. "I've got two guys begging me for that plane."

I worked that week for Sal Paone, and he gave me a one-week advance.

That put me at $180. Two trips to New York equaled $60, and with the $180, I had the $240.

I labor through all of this money stuff to tell any young readers that money doesn't grow on trees. College students are always broke, and they need to remember that they can't depend on family and friends to pull them through. Can you imagine me calling my family and saying, "Can you help me out? I want to buy an old airplane." Yeah, that would have gone over like a lead balloon.

My dad had often said, "If you are smart enough, and want something, you'll figure a way to earn it." And I did. I had an airplane! It may have been a wrung-out Champ, and I might have had to share it with eight other people, but it was mine. I was an airplane owner. I flew the Champ back to Spring Valley, which was located near Nyack College.

Bill and his beloved Champ with Carmen,
his first passenger in that plane

It was a great feeling. Now if I could just log 150 hours in it, and the club members could get 200 hours before the plane needed an overhaul, I'd be okay.

I quit my job at Paone's Pizza later that fall. It was tough taking twenty credit hours, then working, and getting back to the dorm at two a.m.

My NYC camp run ended in the fall, but I kept my school bus run because that money was dedicated to my room and board expenses at college.

By the late spring of the next year, I had my 200 hours; the club was going fine. (As a side note, one of the members of the flying club was a young man named Harold Bowman, who was later martyred in Juba, Sudan, shot by rebels in 1977.) The Champ was holding on, although Bob Shetler, who was the chief mechanic at Spring Valley Airport told me at that time the engine's leak down test told him the engine would not make it to the next inspection. Bob had been Amelia Earhart's mechanic on her Lockheed Electra 10E before she took off on her ill-fated flight across the South Pacific in 1937.

I got the last flight hours out of that engine. I flew everywhere—flying into farmers' fields to visit my farming friends. I flew into every small airport and onto grass strips all over Eastern New York and visited the Aerodrome of First World War fighter planes at the old Rhinebeck Aerodrome every Saturday, weather permitting. The engine finally gave out, so I had it overhauled at Joe Oshinki's shop in New Jersey. I was honing down on my 200 hours.

I had passed my commercial written test and was preparing for my flight exam. The flight exam turned out to be fairly easy. It consisted of flying some lazy eights and chandelles. The maneuvers demonstrate how smoothly a pilot can control the airplane while maintaining correct altitudes and compass headings. But most of the exam was under the hood, a piece of plastic headgear that blocks the pilot's view of everything but the instrument panel, forcing him to fly by instruments only, and to demonstrate his ability to use radio navigation. I passed. Now I could get paid for flying.

Bill Beard, the airport owner, told me that he would schedule me for flights on an as-needed basis. I mostly got sightseeing flights on weekends, flying small groups around Manhattan and the Statue of Liberty. It was easy work, but I wanted more. One Sunday afternoon when I was in my dorm studying (and mostly sleeping), a student got me up saying, "You have a phone call from the airport."

It was the dispatcher at the airport. "We just got a call from a family who said that their father has died while on vacation in Vermont. They want to get his body home as soon as possible. Do you want the flight?"

Did I want it? "I'll be there before you can hang up," I said, and I ran down the hallway hollering, "Anybody want to go along with me on a flight? It will last about four or five hours."

Another student, Donnie Radcliff said he'd go, and we headed to the airport. When we got there, I found that the plane I would be flying was a Piper Cherokee Six—it had 300 HP engine and accommodated six people plus a child. With four seats out and the use of a small cargo door, we would be able to get a casket inside, but it was going to be a tight fit. We climbed in and were off to Rutland, Vermont, about a one-and-a-half-hour flight. We arrived at the airport in Rutland at about five thirty, picked up Mr. Bernstein in his casket, and got back into the air.

I climbed to about 6,000 feet, and all was well. I throttled back to about 2,200 rpm for the cruise home. Just as we were passing over Albany, New York, we could see the glow of New York City on the horizon, and I started my gradual descent for the Spring Valley Airport. Everything was quiet in the plane and Donnie and I were sitting back, watching the glow of the city lights get bigger and bigger. All of a sudden we heard, "Heppp," coming from inside the casket. I looked at Donnie, and his eyes were open wide. Then we heard, "Ugh," and then "ugh," again.

Donnie looked at me and said, "This guy must still be alive!"

"Donnie," I said. "Get the straps off and try to open the lid! This guy needs some air!" Donnie got the casket untied, but the lid could not be opened only a few inches, hitting the cabin overhead.

Mr. Bernstein's voice continued, "Heppp—ugh!"

In desperation, Donnie put his shoe under the lid to hold it open as much as it could. "What are we going to do?" he asked. The nearest airport was about twenty miles away. I called flight service, located at the tower at Duchess County Airport and told him my predicament.

He radioed back and said, "You are cleared for a straight-in approach to runway two-four. I'll have medics standing by for you." As we descended, Mr. Bernstein's voice got louder; as I entered final approach, I could see flashing lights at the south end of the runway. I made a reasonable landing, taxied down the runway and saw a large group of people, an ambulance, and state police waiting for us.

Well, we had quite a tussle getting the casket out of the plane, and when the lid was opened, the coroner dove in with his stethoscope. He hesitated for a moment and then looked up at us and said, "He's dead as a doornail."

"How can that be?" I asked.

"What altitude were you flying at?"

"Sixty-five hundred feet," I answered.

"Well, when you let down, the air compression forced residual air out of his lungs and past his vocal cords, and that was the sound you heard."

Relieved, I could feel my shaking begin to subside. In fact, I started to find the situation humorous, but everyone else had disgusted looks on their faces. The coroner turned back saying, "You made me miss dinner with my family."

The Cherokee Six that Bill and Donnie flew Mr. Bernstein back from Vermont

We stuffed the casket back into the Cherokee and took off for the short hop to Spring Valley. Mr. Bernstein was delivered safely. Safely, but dead.

CHAPTER IX

AVIATION DEVIATION, PART II
THE SILVER DOLLAR

And unto one he gave five talents, to another two, to another one; to each according to his several ability... Straightway he that received the five talents went and traded with them, and made other five talents. In like manner he also that received the two gained other two. But he that received the one went away and digged in the earth, and hid his lord's money (Matthew 25:15-18, ASV).

Lloyd Ballentine was a very big guy, about 6'4" and 250 pounds. He had been my student for about three months. I got him soloed, and checked out for cross country, and was preparing him for his private pilot flight test. One Saturday when he came for his regular lesson, he said he had always wanted to fly a "taildragger" (an early model plane with tailwheel steering, and therefore a more difficult plane to maneuver on the ground as opposed to a "nosewheel" airplane which steers like a car.) Learning to fly a taildragger makes very good pilots. This is because you have to be on the controls every second. You must stay ahead of what is going on by using full travel of the stick and rudder intently to avoid a ground loop or crash landing. If you can master flying a taildragger, particularly in windy conditions, you are considered a "real" pilot. It is like horseback riding—you can't let the horse take you for a ride; you take the horse for a ride by showing him who's boss.

We just happened to have a classic taildragger trainer—a Piper-PA 90 Super Cub 9947 Delta. It was tandem seating (student in the front seat, instructor in the back), stick and rudder controls, front and back, just like my old Champ. But it had a lot more power. I said, "Sure, Lloyd. Let's go!"

I got Lloyd buckled in the front seat, and I climbed into the back. We were all set, but I had not anticipated the effect of Lloyd's size—he totally filled the front cockpit. I couldn't see the instrument panel. Critical gauges like the airspeed indicator and the rpm gauge were out of sight! Well, I thought, we've gone too far to turn back now, and I've flown by the seat of my pants before—I could do it again.

Before takeoff, I told Lloyd, "Just be light on the controls so you can feel what I am doing." I gave full power, the tail came up, and we were off. As I tried to bring the nose up, the controls had locked! The rudders and stick were locked! My student had frozen on the controls, and I couldn't move them an inch. "Lloyd," I yelled, "get off the controls!" He was unmoved, frozen hard on them. The right wing dropped, and we turned, just skimming the rooftops of the airplanes parked along the runway, and heading right for the big plate glass windows of the main office building! I yelled louder, "Get off the controls!" but he remained frozen. I started hitting his head and shoulders. "Get off the controls!" but there was no change. After what seemed like an hour, he finally relaxed, and I yanked the stick back. We missed the airport office by inches but caught the top of a pine tree inside the walls of the Russian convent across the street. I thought we were goners. The engine sputtered but kept running, and I leveled the wings, and we gained altitude. I came around (with several pine branches in the landing gear) and landed!

Bill Beard, the owner/manager of the airport and the entire

staff came running out of the office, and they were mad! Bill was hollering, "What the hell is the matter with you? You almost killed us all!" Of course, there was no concern over what would have happened to Ballentine and me! Everyone on the scene thought that I had been trying to pull some kind of stunt no matter how I tried to explain what had really happened; at that moment I found myself wishing that I had a recording of the panic that had taken place in the cockpit.

Office at Ramapo Airport that Bill and Ballentine almost flew into (Note: awning was up at the time)

Later that afternoon I was reassessing how and why I had gotten into my current situation. I thought back to graduation, most of my friends in the pre-seminary program had gone on to various seminaries. After five years of college life, however, I wanted to take some time off from the intensity of academia. After all, most of the thinkers I had studied came to the wrong conclusions anyway. Aviation, I thought, could provide the respite and adventure I needed. I had attained my commercial rating while in college. The written test and flight examination were fairly routine. The flight instructor's rating, on the other hand, would be a different issue. Although I had studied hard, the written exam took me two and a half hours to complete. Moreover, I was told that the flight test would last between three and four hours, and would include a number of aerobatic maneuvers as well as a preflight oral exam. I would also have to create an elaborate student instructional display book for teaching purposes.

After completing the written part of the test, I focused on flying. I felt comfortable with stalls, spins, and most other flight maneuvers, but the loop eluded me. Either I would fall out on top of the loop and go a spin, or the loop would be egg-shaped rather than circular. I felt myself stressing out. My exam date was coming up, and I still wasn't satisfied with my loop.

Enter Ellery Redfield. Red was a Second World War fighter pilot who, after the war, had instructed in military aircraft for a number of years. I grabbed him one day and asked if he could help me perfect the loop. "Sure," he said. "Let's go up."

I took the Super Cub, and we climbed up to 3,500 feet. "Let's see what you got," he said, and I did my typical messed-up loop ending in a spin.

Red told me to go back up to 3,500 feet and come to a heading of 030, about north on the compass, and I did. He then took a silver dollar out of his pocket and told me to put it on top of the instrument panel. So I placed it right next to the magnetic compass. "Keep your hands and feet light on the controls and follow me through," he instructed. He put the Cub into a dive, pulled the stick full back and planted it there and added full power. I felt him use a little right rudder to compensate for the "p" factor (prop torque that pulls the plane to the left.) in order to maintain the proper heading. Keeping the wings level at all times, he took the plane back through our original altitude of 3,500 feet to about 4,000 feet upside down. He put carburetor heat on. As we descended, power off, we went back through 3,500 feet, sticks full back, to about 3,000 feet, and he added full power to 3,500 feet, leveled off, and powered to a cruise speed of about 2,300 rpm. Heading was exactly 030. The silver dollar had not budged an inch, even though we were upside down! A perfect loop!

But, I wondered, could I do that? Red let me practice two or three times. I did a reasonable job, and we headed back to the field. I only had one week to practice before my flight exam. I was hoping for perfect conditions, but when the day came it was a bit windy, and my examiner was about two hours late. I was getting nervous. When he finally arrived, we went through the oral exam in the coffee shop; it took about forty-five minutes. My FAA examiner, a short, gruff man, never commented on anything. We got into the plane and went up to about 3,000 feet. He had me do basic air work, power-off and power-on stalls, right and left spins. And then came the dreaded loop. I went step-by-step as if Ellery Redfield was there. It was a good loop, although I leveled off ten degrees off my entry heading. But he couldn't see the compass from the back seat. "Let's go back to the field," he said.

On the downwind leg, he pulled the mixture out, turning off the engine. "Now," he instructed, "put it on the numbers," referring to the large numbers painted at the end of the runway, designating the compass heading.

I pulled the carb heat on and thought, "This is where a hundred hours in the Champ will pay off. I've done this over fifty times." I pulled a full-stall landing right on the numbers!

And all he said was, "That's all. Park it." No other comment. As we walked back to the office in eerie silence, he suddenly said, "You must have had a good instructor."

"Yes, sir," I answered. "Very good."

"You know you were off ten degrees from your heading after the loop."

"Yes, sir," I said, but I wondered. My body blocked his view of the instruments. How could he know that? I learned later that he used a checkpoint on the horizon before we entered the loop.

"Who was your instructor?" he asked.

I replied, "Ellery Redfield was one of the best." And with that, he told me that I had passed. I was now certified flight instructor #1682771CI.

As soon as the following day, I had students booked. The flying crowd, like other small groups of enthusiasts—car clubs, horse fanatics, sports clubs, etc. has its share of characters. We were no exception. There was Bernie Horowitz, a really nice guy but very accident-prone. He parked and refueled airplanes for the airport. Bernie would always have a sympathy-inspiring story to explain his latest bandage. The final episode of Bernie's career was when he got his hand caught in the large fan of an airplane pre-heater and lost a finger. Responding to his cries, I got him into my truck and was rushing him to the local hospital when I realized we didn't have the severed finger. When we reached the hospital, I called Paul Shafer, our head mechanic, who found it in the debris that littered the hangar floor and rushed it to the emergency room, where the doctor was able to clean it and stitch it back on.

Then there was Dr. Eric Rothschild, a truly gracious guy. He gave our instructors their annual physicals for free! However, as any flight instructor knows, doctors and most professional men make the worst student pilots—they always know better than the instructor. That makes teaching them very frustrating and difficult. And as fine a man as Dr. Rothschild was, he was no exception. Three instructors threw their hands up and then gave him to me. I fared no better; in fact, it was a joke around the field that every landing with Rothschild was a crash landing. If you walked away from it, it was a good landing. His generosity, however, made up for our frustrations. He bought a brand new Piper 180 Cherokee fully equipped N-454 MD (medical doctor) and gave his flight instructors a key to use it whenever we wanted—dinner with a date, Atlantic City, Martha's Vineyard for a swim. It was great.

Finally, there was Don Swann. Don was a braggart, always talking about how financially well off he was. And who were we to doubt? After all, he drove a Cadillac! However, we all began to wonder why, after lunch with Don, we always got stuck with the check. He was the one who claimed he was loaded. I understood a little better when, after an engagement dinner for my fiancée, Kathleen, and me, the Swanns gave us a gift—a small appliance for making toasted sandwiches. When Kath unwrapped the box, she found a card that said, "From Betty to Barbara Collins." Strange. But there was another envelope with a card saying, "From Barbara to my best friend, Elizabeth." Finally, we opened the card that had been taped to the box. It read, "To Bill and Kathy from Don and Elizabeth Swann." Apparently, the present had not been opened fully in its passage from Betty to Barbara to Elizabeth to us. That said all we needed to know about the wealthy Swanns.

There were many other airport characters like Bob Collins who was so proud of his old World War II "Navion," an old rattletrap that we had to go pick parts of it off the runway whenever he took off and landed. We always worried that he might fly out and not return. And there were others. My experiences as a flight instructor could fill another book.

A few months after I received my instructor's rating, Bill Beard, the owner of Ramapo Airport, called me and invited me to lunch. After settling down in a booth at the local diner, Bill told me that he was getting tired of the flight school business and wanted to concentrate on aircraft sales. He said that he would sell me five trainers (Cessna 150s) for $45,000 each, for a total of $225,000, and he would throw in the Super Cub if I wanted the deal. He also offered a large Quonset hut at no rental charge on the field to use for office space, maintenance, and aircraft storage. What a deal! But what would I do?

I really wanted to go back to school and work on my master's degree, using my instructor's rating to earn income. I hadn't considered any other options. But then I remembered something my father had told me. "The greatest gift anyone can give you is an opportunity." I also thought of my Biblical studies. Jesus was the ultimate compassionate capitalist. He fed the hungry, healed the sick and lame, and blessed the one who used an opportunity to make a profit for his master (Matthew 25:15-25). Maybe, I thought to myself, I could build a successful business and do something for the kingdom? Wrong thinking. In Matthew 25, Jesus gave an opportunity to His servants. I was not yet a servant, but this was still a great opportunity.

One problem still presented itself—I had no money and no credit, a major problem. But I did have a student named John Jones, who was Vice President at Nanuet National Bank, and another student, whose name I can no longer remember, who was a stockbroker on Wall Street. This student was close friends with a wealthy investment broker named John C. Traphagen. If Jones would give me a loan and Traphagen would guarantee it, I would go ahead with Beard's offer. Today when I think back on it, what a crazy scheme! What banker would give a loan of over $200,000 to a young man with no business experience, and what man in his right mind would guarantee a $200,000 loan to a man he doesn't even know?

I wondered if I should even pursue the issue further. But then on my next lesson with John Jones, I ran Bill Beard's offer by him. "Listen, John," I said, "I have a connection with an investment broker, John Traphagen who might consider guaranteeing your loan."

"Well, Bill," John said. "Get me Traphagen's financial statement, and I'll go ahead with the proposal." One step taken care of.

When my Wall Street student came for his next lesson, I told him of the plan and said that I had the financing if his man would guarantee it. My student answered that he would give the idea a try. I did not hear from him for two weeks, and I began to think that he had forgotten about our conversation, or maybe Traphagen had rejected the whole idea.

And then, out of the blue, I got a message to call him back. "Mr. Traphagen would like to meet you." Well, that was a new pressure. How was I to prepare for such a meeting? I had never met a multimillionaire before.

My student picked me up one evening at the airport; we drove to Mr. Traphagen's estate on the Hudson River where I met with him in his library. A tall, thin man, he was younger than I had expected—late forties or early fifties perhaps. He spent some time questioning me about my past—my family, the farm, the Marine Corps, and my college education. And then he got down to why I wanted to get into the aviation business and particularly why I wanted his help. We talked for about forty-five minutes, and then, after a short pause, he answered me using a term that has stuck with me to this day—he said, "I see that you are a 'straight' young man" (That word, straight, in Hebrew is "*yashar*" which is interpreted as "righteous" as it refers to God.) I understood it as a true compliment certainly beyond my grasp, but one that would be a challenge to live up to, too. Then he concluded, "Have your banker call me tomorrow." Pleasantries were exchanged, and we left.

John Jones called me the following day and said, "The deal is closed. Come by later and sign the paperwork." And Span Air was born.

I lassoed three of my students to help me get started: Barbara Brague as bookkeeper, secretary, and schedule keeper. I had great confidence in her. She had been my first female student, very bright and determined. She soloed in seven hours, one of only two of my students to do so. Johnny Pollack was a bright college student whose job was to take care of our airplanes—tie them down in the evening, pull them out in the morning, fuel them, and check them out, getting them ready to fly. Jim Meile was the third hire. He was our certified mechanic who would do twenty-five-hour inspections and the general maintenance needed to keep the planes flying. And then there was me, "jack of all trades" and the only instructor. Also, I have to give credit to Eddie Edvardsen, my student and carpenter and the Gros family for helping me get Span Air flying.

Bill and Lynn Gross, age sixteen (youngest student to get private pilot's license at Span Air) with Super Cub 9947D, flown in Silver Dollar, Ballentine, and Woodstock episodes.

CHAPTER X

AVIATION DEVIATION, PART III
NEVER A DULL MOMENT

If I ascend up into heaven, thou art there: If I make my bed in Sheol, behold, thou art there. If I take the wings of the morning, And dwell in the uttermost parts of the sea; Even there shall thy hand lead me, And thy right hand shall hold me (Psalm 139:8-10, ASV).

Our business motto was "Enjoy the Freedom of Flight." And it caught on—so well in fact, that in a short period of time I had seven full-time instructors and three part-time instructors for the weekend overload. I expanded the training fleet by purchasing four Piper 140s. The flying school was growing, and then to add to that business, the air charter business exploded. Orange and Rockland Power called wanting me to fly power line patrol. It seemed hunters were shooting electric insulators at the O&R towers in the Ramapo Mountains. So every morning I'd fly low over the Ramapos in the Super Cub with a camera, checking the towers. Then a local radio station called, wanting me to fly an air traffic route, reporting live on traffic congestion on the Major Deegan Expressway and the Tappan Zee Bridge, every day between four and six p.m. Also, several owners of large estates wanted us to fly observation patrols around their homes daily while they wintered in Florida.

Eventually, we also signed two lucrative charter contracts—one with Lederle Labs to fly pharmaceuticals to points in the

Northeast and one with the *New York Times* to fly manuscripts for printing to their Dayton, Ohio plant. The latter was for $100,000 over a six-month period, and I had to buy an all-weather twin Piper Aztec to facilitate the contract. A new Cherokee Six 300 and a twin-engine Piper followed, to help with instrument flight instruction and other charters.

Piper Twin Apache
Purchased to give multi-engine and instrument instruction.

In addition to these business contracts, I also had my regular flying lessons. Each student had their own story, but there was one student, however, whom I was most proud of, and that I will never forget. I feel this story is worth telling. Looking at the flight schedule each day, I noticed the name Leonard Billy. He regularly flew with my flight instructor, Tom Settani. I always noticed his name because I thought it should be Billy Leonard. Billy shouldn't be his last name, but it was. Well, time went by, and I began to ignore his name, but one day Tom came to me and said he couldn't do anymore for Leonard. "What is the problem?" I asked.

"Billy is mentally challenged, and has a serious learning difficulty," he answered, "and even after forty hours flying with him, I don't think he will ever get it." Then he asked me to fly with Billy for evaluation and then counsel him to take up a less-demanding hobby. So I agreed.

I saw immediately how deep Leonard's problems were. Afterward, we went to the Pilot's Lounge coffee shop where I explained to Billy that not everybody could be a pilot. I pointed out to him that he had already spent three times what the average pilot takes to solo and he still had a long way to go before he would be ready. (I was thinking that the idea of not wasting money might soften the blow.) Then Billy told me his story. "I know I'm not smart," he said. "I live with my mom, but I spend all day in a group home for mentally disabled people" He continued, "All I talked about was how I was going to become a pilot. But all my friends mocked and laughed at me and said, 'You're stupid,' 'you're too dumb,' 'you'll never be a pilot.'" He had tears in his eyes. I put my head down and thought for a long time.

Finally, I lifted my head, and looked at him. "Leonard, you are going to become a pilot. Let's get started!"

After twenty more hours, my frustrations began to overwhelm me. Every lesson was simply a review of what we had done before. I couldn't get to new items because he was unable to retain what we had last gone over. The whole key to learning to fly is conquering things as they are learned, and making them habits so you can go on to more difficult tasks like controlling airspeed, direction, rpm, and flare to landing.

After an additional ten hours, I realized that I was going to have to change my method of instruction. I knew Billy was never going to get the "feel" of flying. Most students, when they know the routine, the sequence of actions they must perform, develop a "feel" or sensation for what the airplane is doing. With my students on final approach, I often covered the airspeed indicator and say "Maintain eighty" to see if they had the "feel" of the plane. We call this "flying by the seat of our pants"—all good pilots have a sense of this, even airline pilots. But sometimes a man with above average intelligence like Eric Rothschild did not get it, and I knew Leonard Billy never would, so I decided to change to a rote method of teaching. I figured if I could get Billy to memorize just seven things, he'd be a pilot.

This new method, called "mechanical flying," was not the best way to fly but my hope here was that it would work for Leonard Billy. First I took the seven steps and divided them into three parts. I thought three would be easier to memorize. Part "A": Bring the plane to altitude; Part "B": prepare to land; Part "C": landing the plane. So here goes Billy.

Step #1: After preflight, line up the plane on the center of the runway; slowly add full power and slight backpressure on the controls; maintain eighty-five mph.

Step #2: Make a shallow ninety-degree turn over the Thruway; maintain eighty-five mph.

Step #3: Make another shallow bank left turn over the shopping mall, bring power back to cruise speed (relax). This was part "A" next.

Step #4 (the middle step, prepare to land): When equal to the end of the runway, carb heat on; bring power back to 1500 rpm; maintain eighty mph. This ended part "B."

Step #5: Make ninety-degree left turn over Korvett's store; maintain eighty mph.

Step #6: Make another ninety-degree left turn over the church; maintain eighty mph.

Step #7: Line up with the runway; add power if low; reduce power if high; maintain eighty at all times. When one foot off the runway put carb heat off; cut the power and land the plane. (I couldn't teach Billy the use of flaps; I thought it would be too confusing.)

Three parts, seven steps: 1, 2, 3—4—5, 6, 7. Could he memorize it?

Now let me insert here—Spring Valley was a very difficult place to learn to fly. The runway was only 2800 feet long, and if your wheels were not down on the runway in the first 500 feet, you needed to take off and go around to set up another approach. That is why the approach was so important. If you came in too high, you would land too far down the runway to stop, and you would run out of runway. I put a red cone about 500 feet up the runway and told my students, "If you are not down by that cone, go around and set up another approach. When you are a foot off the runway, cut power and land the plane."

Ramapo Valley Airport, also known as Spring Valley Airport, with its 2800-foot runway.

I knew this was not the best method, but given a perfectly calm day, Billy could do it without me. So we continued. I had him memorizing the steps day and night. I'd call him during the day. "Billy, give me the steps." Before we went flying, "Repeat the steps."

One day Billy came to me and said, "I have to quit. I am out of money. My mother said it was ridiculous to keep trying to learn to fly. 'You'll never be able to fly!' I can't give you any more money."

Well, I owned the airplane and was donating my time, so let's keep going. After about another twenty hours of memorizing, memorizing, memorizing, I told my staff and instructors that if I got a perfect day the following week, I was going to solo Leonard Billy. The reactions ranged from, "You are crazy," to my secretary saying, "Tell me when you are going to attempt this so I can have an ambulance on standby!"

The next Thursday was a nice summer day, and at around seven p.m. the weather was perfectly calm. The time had come. Billy gave me three reasonable landings. "Billy," I said, "I'm going to solo you. Do a landing exactly like you did the last one." I got out of the plane at the end of the runway. It seemed like the whole airport came out to watch.

As Leonard pushed the throttle in, I prayed, "Oh Lord, please don't let anything go wrong." He flew a perfect mathematically arranged pattern. I prayed again, "Lord, please squish Murphy's Law." His approach was a little high, but okay if it didn't carry him too far down the runway. He flared, landed a little long, but safely and came to a stop!

We were all cheering and jumping up and down. Billy was too nervous to taxi the plane to the ramp, so one of my instructors had to do it for him. Leonard Billy was a pilot! We had a little ceremony afterward, and I presented him with a set of lapel wings, as well as a certificate signed by me with the date, the place, and the airplane he had flown.

I never saw Billy again. All he had wanted was to show his friends that he was a pilot and he did. Good job, Billy!

There was an incident when I was flying in the pattern with a student. My secretary called me on the unicom (radio). "Get down here quickly," she said. "There's a man here in a panic to see you." So I cut short my lesson, landed, and parked the plane. He came running down. It was August 15, 1969. He said, "My fifteen-year-old daughter is with some hippies in Woodstock. I need to rescue her today. If she stays overnight, she'll lose her virginity. I've hired two detectives, and they've got her, but no ground transportation can get anywhere near there. I've gone to three airports to rent a helicopter, but they're all busy going up there. Can you help?" Well, I had the Super Cub and have flown in and out of many farmer's fields, so I said I would give it a try. I took off. In forty-five minutes I saw a sea of people, about 1,000 yards wide and long. I looked for a field and saw two, one a long field but somewhat far away. The shorter pasture was closer but tricky to land in. I would have to lean hard on my brakes. I buzzed the concert so the detectives would see me and set up for a landing on the shorter pasture. I did a slow flight pass over the field to check for woodchuck holes. They could be a disaster. There were a lot of helicopters buzzing around, so I had to be very careful. I landed. Sure enough, the two detectives came across the field, one handcuffed to a petite young lady. I wouldn't have to be worried about being overloaded. I felt sorry for her being strapped into my flimsy Super Cub. It must have been frightening. I taxied to the end of the field, gave the Cub full power, and we were off the ground within 300 feet. She didn't say anything when I tried to start a conversation. She just had fear in her eyes. Forty-five minutes later, I had her back in the arms of her thankful father.

Although this was a one-shot deal, we had many other crazy flights. For example, later after I was married, I went home for lunch one Sunday. Just as I was sitting down with Kathleen to eat my tuna fish sandwich, I got a call from Johnny Pollack. "You'd better get back here right now. There's a man upstairs in your office praying. I think he is crazy." I darted back to the airport as fast as my '67 Mustang could take me. Sure enough, there was a short, stocky man on his knees, praying. His name was Mr. Keck. His story was that he needed to get to Rochester as soon as possible. Driving up the Thruway, he saw airplanes flying around when an angel told him to park his car, and if he went up over the hill, a silver bird would fly him to Rochester. So he parked his car (right on the highway) and walked through the woods to our office. I checked the distance up and back and said it would cost about $300. Well, he had plenty of money. There was one problem. It was a Sunday, and all my planes were flying with students. I had one plane not being used. It was the seven-passenger Cherokee Six. So we strapped Mr. Keck in, and Kathleen and I took off. As we gained altitude out of Ramapo, I saw Keck's Cadillac parked in the right lane of the Thruway with five or six police cars with flashing lights around it. Well, we got to altitude and adjusted the VOR on a radial to Rochester. About thirty minutes into the flight, Kathleen and I heard a "sheek, sheek" scraping sound coming from where Mr. Keck was sitting. I told Kathleen to see what he was doing. She said, "He's dry shaving with a straight razor and singing the Lord's Prayer."

I said, "Keep an eye on him, that he doesn't cut his throat."

Well, we landed in Rochester, and I was glad to get him out of my plane. We headed back to Ramapo. The story didn't end there. On Monday afternoon, I got a call from Mr. Keck. He was naked in a phone booth in Albany, New York, and wanted me to come and get him! I said, "Mr. Keck, I can't land my plane on Main Street in Albany. Can you get to the airport?" The phone went dead. I called the local police and reported the car incident. I never heard from Mr. Keck again but prayed that he would be all right.

As if this didn't keep me busy enough (seventeen hours a

day or more), I had to learn how to run a business. When I got started, I didn't even know about payroll taxes, social security taxes, and workmen's comp, much less how to maintain profit and loss statements, read a balance sheet, or make up a financial spreadsheet. All of this I had to learn on the fly by trial and error. It was overwhelming, but it was all about to change when I connected with one of my new students, Irwin Lampert.

CHAPTER XI

SPAN EAST AIRLINES AND WEDDING BELLS

And we know that all things work together for good to them that love God, to them who are the called according to his purpose. For whom he did fore-know, he also did predestinate to be conformed to the image of his Son, that he might be the firstborn among many brethren (Romans 8:28-29, KJV).

I was returning one night from a charter flight in the Twin Aztec. It was a crystal clear, calm CAVU (ceiling and visibility unlimited) night. I had just gotten the engines in sync and stopped the props from oscillating. Everything was quiet, the engines humming. I turned on the autopilot, sat back to monitor the instruments. I had time to contemplate and think; why had my little flying school grown from five planes and one instructor to eighteen planes and twelve instructors in less than two years? Why had we gone from rarely having a single charter flight a month to running two or three a day?

My mind went back to the obstacle course of my early Marine days. There I had learned some secrets about life. Not only do you have to show up early and stay late, but you have to know how to aggressively and relentlessly handle obstacles. A ten-foot wall is not easy to get over, especially without help. But I found that running at it at an angle, springing off the bracing helped me get my fingers on the top board, then with a little oomph, I was over. Getting a loan for over $200,000 was not an easy obstacle to overcome, but a strategy of boldness, humility, honesty, and planning opened that door. I learned from my dad and the obstacle course that if you want the rewards from any job or visionary enterprise, you can't play it safe; you have to attack it with all your mind and physical strength—you need to do it with all your might.

The next morning I saw a new student on my schedule—Irwin Lampert. Irwin was a short Jewish lawyer—neat, good looking, and personable. He was also a certified public accountant. We hit it off right away and struck up a close friendship. I taught him to fly, and he taught me everything about keeping proper books, creating financial statements, and drawing up contracts. After about two months, he and his wife, Judy, and I went out to dinner, and over dessert, Irwin said, "You have a very good business going with Span Air. If you could spin off the air charter business, I think we could raise some money, buy another airline, and enter the big-time."

Surprised, I asked, "How could we raise that kind of money?"

"A public offering," he answered. "We'll take Span Air public!"

Well, that was certainly above my pay grade. I didn't know anything about the world of high finance—I was strictly a stick and rudder jock. But the idea was intriguing. "Irwin," I asked, "what would you want in return?"

"Ten percent of the company," was his answer.

That night I sat and thought about his proposal. This was huge. And a guy who could pull off a miracle of that magnitude was certainly entitled to a ten-percent stake. The next morning when I saw Irwin, I said without hesitation, "Let's go!"

And he was ready. He got Robert Cea and Company to take us public. After filing a prospectus with S.E.C. (Security and Exchange Commission), Cea offered 75,000 shares of stock in Span Air at $4.00 a share. This grossed $300,000; after a commission to Cea of $40,000, the company netted $226,000 dollars.

(left) Announcing public offering,
(right) Promoting Span Air flying school

At the same time, Universal Airlines, a freight airline out of Ypsilanti, Michigan, was offering to sell its entire piston fleet of five DC 6s and ten C-46s for one million dollars. They would also include an eight-million-dollar contract to fly automotive freight with the purchase. We signed the deal.

Now I want to say something about these airplanes. The C-46 was the big brother of the DC-4 (the DC was for McDonald Douglas—cargo), the same planes that I flew on when I was in Germany during the Berlin Airlift in '48 and '49. The C-46 was the original Commando that became famous for flying over the Himalaya Mountains, a route named "the Hump," to fly supplies to the British and Chinese troops that were fighting the Japanese in China in the late 30s and early 40s. The DC-6 could carry about 30,000 pounds or fifteen tons, of freight, while the C-46 was able to carry 15,000 pounds or seven and a half tons. Both planes had Pratt and Whitney R-2800 engines, rated at 2000 horsepower each. These Pratt and Whitney eighteen-cylinder twin row radials were the best made at that time. "Piston-engine perfection," wrote Stephen Wilkinson of the R-2800 (*Aviation History*, March 2009, p. 32). (However, the turboprop was becoming popular and the Boeing 707 was soon to be introduced. I knew we had a lot of problems to "keep 'em flying," but I thought later that we could trade up to more modern aircraft.)

R-2800 Pratt and Whitney eighteen-cylinder engine.
Span East had fifty-five of these great engines.
(photo credits: Air Classics Magazine)

Now with our increased business, my payroll went from $6,000 a week to $60,000 a week as my staff went from twenty-five to 150. My hanger and office space went from 5,000 sq.

ft. to over 40,000 sq. ft. I consider my time and experience in aviation a Masters if not a Ph.D. in business, human relations, and common sense. That education enabled me to make the sacrifices that would be necessary for ministry later on.

We formed a subsidiary of Span Air called Span East Airlines. We started flying freight daily to all major cities in the U.S. from Willow Run Airport in Ypsilanti. I now spent my time, three days a week managing the flight school in Spring Valley and three days managing Span East in Michigan. On Sundays, I tried to be home. I attended the First Baptist Church in Nanuet where Pastor Leslie Flynn was preaching. Pastor Flynn was a great guy who at that time had authored seven books, mostly on practical Christian living. The people of the congregation were warm and very friendly. Arminian dispensationalism was on the back burner there—I didn't hear a word about it, and I thought, "This is the way a church should be, concentrating on communicating the gospel and not on promoting questionable doctrines."

Flashback one year to 1967. My stepbrother, Rodger, would come up from Florida to visit friends during the summer, and while he was here, he drove buses and would fly with me when we had time. On one of those trips, he was introduced to a girl named Carol through Bonnie Rutherford, a close family friend. They dated and got engaged and planned to marry that April. He asked me to be his best man, and at a post-reception party at Carol's parents' house, I met her cousin, Kathleen. At the first meeting, I felt she was someone special. She was in her junior year at West Chester State College in Pennsylvania. After a few dates, I fell in love, but she was in college, and I was in the throes of increasing activities at Span Air. On her weekends home and over the summer we would often fly out to airport restaurants like the Flying W Ranch or the restaurant at Westchester County Airport. At other times we would take off in the Super Cub and visit my friends from my farming days in Sussex County. I would circle the farms, find a field close to the house and barns, check the wind direction, and land. Kathy and I shared a love of farms and cows, and we had great times.

Everyone I knew suspected I was very serious about Kathy when I nicknamed her Charley, the name of my beloved horse from my farming days. Charley it was! She was the apple of my eye. Soon after that at a Chinese restaurant, I asked her to marry me. And she said no! Rejected, I decided not to ask her again. We continued to date from time to time, but she had graduation coming up, and I was in the thick of my public offering and organizing Span East airlines. Charley and I dated on and off for the next several months, but she had other boy interests at that time. I understood that—we were ten years apart, and she was just out of college. About six months went by and on a date one night she said she would marry me. We got engaged, and then, on November 2, 1968, we got married in a little Episcopal church in her hometown. We exchanged the traditional vows— she to love, honor and obey, and I to cherish her as Christ did the church.

We moved into the Bon Aire Apartments in Suffern, NY. Charley taught sixth grade at the State Street School in Hackensack, New Jersey, and made a good income while I, from the beginning of Span Air, only took home eighty dollars a week as to not burden the company.

As Span East developed, the freight airline made approximately four million in 1970. Most of the money went to pay off the airplanes and the balance to operational costs. However, we were able to net $8000 that year. I got a raise. Things were booming in the freight business in '70 and '71. But at that time two problems developed. First, as the overall finances grew and demanded more and more professional attention. I appointed

Irwin president, so he had the title to deal with those issues. Secondly, we flew piston aircraft in a turbo and jet-age world. The FAA (Federal Aviation Agency) was all over us. Every week there were inspections. I had to devote my full time to this issue. I had forty R-2800 engines on airplanes and fifteen in overhaul. I was rotating about eight engines a month. It was challenging, but our crew got it done. It may have been the jet age, but there was nothing like the sound of four R-2800s at full throttle when taking off.

Our planes would line up and the flight line at eleven p.m. The ground crew would load automotive freight (car parts) from General Motors and Ford. The planes would take off at one a.m. The DC 6s would fly to the major cities (Los Angeles, Dallas, Atlanta, Miami, and Newark). The C-46s would fly to smaller cities all over the U.S. as scheduled. The freight would then be distributed to automotive dealers in their regions—24-hour delivery!

Things were truly booming; we could hardly keep up with it. But unforeseen changes were in the wind.

Charley became pregnant, and on June 4, 1970, she delivered a son—William Henry Spanjer IV. I was elated and raised a flag announcing, "It's a boy!" outside the Span office. Now, Charley had great parents, Hap and Kay Bartels living in Oradell, New Jersey, about twenty minutes from Spring Valley and she and Billy went to live there while we were making preparations to move to a farm.

Charley and I had determined not to raise a family in the crowded, stuffy, traffic-congested suburbs of Rockland County, New York. We spent every weekend driving all over Sussex County, New Jersey, and Orange County, New York, looking for a small farm. We finally set our eyes on a farm located on a dirt road and surrounded by woods with no neighbors in sight. It had several barns, silos, a three-acre pond, and a picturesque stream flowing through the property. It had been a dairy farm dating back to the late 1700s. Ideal!

The property was about one hour from Span Air's office in Spring Valley and had a 3800-foot field behind the house that was suitable for a landing strip. What more could I ask for? The only problem was that the farm was 262 acres and priced at $125,000. I had no available money—only a large debt. I didn't look good on paper; it was inconceivable that a bank would give me a loan. Even if I just wanted to buy it as a "farmette"—ten acres, the barns, and house—the price would be over $60,000. I tried every angle, with no success. The financial obstacles were too high for us to get over. I was concerned that we would lose the deal—there were other buyers waiting in the wings.

On our way to Ypsilanti in the Aztec, I talked the situation over with Irwin. "Look, Bill," he said. "Let's buy the whole farm. I've got a client who will put up the down payment. We'll all sign the mortgage, and we'll have a three-way partnership. You can live in the house and farm the property." So we did it.

I spent the next month fixing up the old farmhouse so that Charley and little Billy would move in. One of my students, a Norwegian builder, Eddie Edvardsen, and I worked day and night on it when I could get time off from the business. The house was a mess. The original farmhouse, built in 1808 had burned down in 1909, almost killing the owner, the father of Bill Fleury, whom I would later meet. The elder Fleury did eventually succumb to his injuries, I was told. The present house was built around 1910 on the same site.

Charley, Billy and I moved in on August 10, 1970. I was still, however, spending three days a week in Michigan, and Charley was alone on a dirt road, on a farm in the woods with no other house in sight. Besides that, our phone was on a party line with several other families. The phone was practically unusable.

Just as everything was going great at Span Air, Span East, and the farm, storm clouds were gathering. Lightning was about to strike. Bill Beard, the owner of Ramapo Valley Airport, decided to allow another flight school, Ram Air, to set up on the field. Ramapo Aviation came in with big money, brand new airplanes, and massive advertising. In a short time, Span Air's business was cut in half. Using the increase in our last couple of years at the flight school as a sign of growth to come, we had purchased four additional airplanes, taking on a quarter million dollars more in debt. I had not seen this overwhelming competition coming. I was stunned. And then, as I tried to figure out how we would adjust to the situation we now faced. We learned that the UAW (United Auto Workers union) was about to strike the automotive industry. The question was—which of the Big Three automakers would they strike—Ford, Chrysler, or General Motors? Now, at that time GM gave us ninety percent of our freight business. I stayed glued to the radio every day, and our employees were on edge. Which company would it be? Then, on September 14, 1970, they announced that they would strike GM. All of my R-2800's went dead. We couldn't afford to fly them only ten percent loaded. Now the question was, how long would the strike last?

Two problems loomed. First, planes that sit and don't fly create a maintenance nightmare. Radios don't work because of moisture that gets in them, electrical systems begin to fail, and hydraulic systems begin to leak. We estimated that if the planes sat for over thirty days, it would cost our company $5000 per plane to get them back in flying condition again.

Secondly, the FAA had a crazy rule that if pilots get laid off for more than thirty days, they would have to go back to school for retraining. This would cost an additional $10,000 per pilot.

With our crew of twenty-five pilots, this would cost over a quarter million dollars. With that in mind, and with no income and limited funds in the bank, we thought we could keep the pilots on the payroll for thirty days. But how long would the strike last? Initially, we were told it would be "only a few days." I tried to keep a few planes flying in the Caribbean. We flew fabric for a company called Her Majesty to Mayaguez, Puerto Rico, for manufacturing—they made Van Heusen shirts. We also got a contract to fly frozen chicken to Port-au-Prince, Haiti, for a restaurant chain. This, however, only took one plane and four pilots. The strike went on for sixty-seven days, and when it was over the automotive companies had given so much to the UAW that priority air freight never recovered. We were finished. If we couldn't "keep 'em flying," then we couldn't pay our debt.

A side note. All charter carriers (airlines) flew under FAA Rules 121. We all (and there were many) have to have contracts with other companies to fly. This, as opposed to common carriers who can fly anytime and anywhere, known as scheduled airlines, like American and United Airlines. There was a bill before Congress to deregulate the airlines. We would no longer need contracts to fly. All 121 carriers tried to hang on until this law passed. Then we could upgrade and try to compete with the big boys. Well, the next year, the industry was deregulated. This inspired the development of regional lines and national carriers like US Airlines and gave birth to UPS and FedEx.

We couldn't make it. Now it would take big-time financing to hold us over until more contracts or deregulation came through. Irwin said that he found a person who would put up the funding. However, he wanted me out. He wanted to buy all of my shares and take control of the company. He did not offer me any money, but he would take over all the debt obligations on Span East. I would get rid of over $2,000,000 of debt. They also did not want the assets of Span Air; they only wanted the name because it was the public company. I was distraught. I was losing the flight school and the airline. I guess it was the saddest flight of my life when I took the Aztec back to Spring Valley for the last time.

The final blow came when Bill Beard decided to sell the airport to a shopping center developer. It was over. I sold most of the school airplanes to cover the debt on them. John Traphagen was off the hook. I took my staff to Pascack Inn (a great hangout for our company) and thanked them for all their dedicated work and said goodbye.

It was hard to see everything working out "for good" after losing everything I had poured my heart and soul in for the last five years. But I knew that I loved God; as to being "called according to His purposes," that I wasn't sure of. However, that issue would be solved shortly. God was driving me back to my roots; my aviation deviation was over. I was sad to leave aviation; it was a wonderful experience. Unbeknownst to me, a greater experience lay ahead. God's providence was leading me back to the farm.

Span East Airlines DC6 getting ready to receive cargo at Ypsilanti Airport

CHAPTER XII

CRISIS IN FARM COUNTRY

For every beast of the forest is mine, and the cattle upon a thousand hills. I know all the birds of the mountains; and the wild beasts of the field are mine. If I were hungry, I would not tell thee; for the world is mine, and the fulness thereof (Psalm 50:10-12, ASV).

I closed the flight school, sold the airplanes and paid all of the debts that were outstanding. I could not reach some students who had given money in advance (block time), so I reserved some funds if they tried to get in touch with me. The Aztec and the Super Cub were free and clear of debt, so I took them with me. I parked the Aztec at Orange County Airport and the Cub at the farm. Charley, Billy, and I made several trips to Florida in the twin to see my dad and the family. This was a great way to travel. We would have an early breakfast at our farm, then leave Orange County Airport about nine a.m., have lunch, and refuel at noon in Norfolk, Virginia. We'd get to Dad's farm in Dunnellon, Florida about four thirty p.m., land in a field at a neighbor's farm, take a swim, and then sit down for dinner with the family at six p.m. Now that was the way to do it. It was a true benefit from the sale of Span East.

Well, now I was back on the farm, with a family to feed and a mortgage to pay. We had no income, but I had 262 acres to farm. The laws had changed. It would be too expensive to go into dairy farming again. The barns were too old to remodel; doing so would not be cost-effective. But there were about 150 acres of lay land. Two cuttings of hay would bring in about $18,000, and there was enough land left to support a small herd of beef cattle. To follow that plan, I visited farm sales and picked up some older John Deere tractors, as well as a 14T hay baler, three flat wagons, a seven-foot sickle bar three-point hitch mower and a Nicholson hay tedder (the best hay tedder ever made—I got it for $250). I was on my way to being a farmer again. In June 1972, Charley gave birth to our second son, who we named Daniel Ralph, after my uncle.

Bailing hay
My oldest son, Bill, driving the
John Deere 620 pulling 14T
bailer; my third son, Tim, stack-
ing hay bales on a flat wagon.

Bill cutting hay with
John Deere 520

A brief flashback. My uncle, Ralph, was a major general in the Marine Corps and a man I had admired all my life. In one incident, he saved my butt at Parris Island. After graduation, all of my platoon mates had gotten their orders and shipped out. Only I was left with Womack— not pleasant. Ralph, who was a colonel at the time, flew up from Florida in a Corsair to Parris Island and found us in the PX picking up the platoon pictures. To Womack's shock, Ralph went to headquarters to straighten things out. Womack later said, "Why didn't you tell me that your uncle was a colonel in the Corps?" I answered him by saying, "I didn't want any special treatment." I got my orders that afternoon, and I was on my way to meet Bob Hoppe at Camp LeJeune.

Maj. Gen. Ralph Spanjer, USMC, with President Ronald Regan and First Lady Nancy Regan

Now, years after my time in the Marine Corps and aviation, I was starting on a new path. I still had God on my mind, as well as a heart open to finding His plans for my life. I counted my aviation deviation as building blocks to my future ministry. I was free from the previous daily responsibilities, and I could take the time to focus on what God would have me do. Although I had had a good experience at First Baptist in Nanuet, I still did not want to be involved in an Arminian Dispensational Church. So we decided to attend a local RCA Church (Reformed Church in America). Now I knew that Presbyterians had deep roots in the Reformation but must have gone liberal when neo-orthodoxy came to America. But we thought we would try. Rev. Dorr Van Etten was an elderly gentleman who had graduated before his seminary became liberal. He was a great gospel preacher who believed the Bible to be the inspired word of God. He and I had many good conversations in his study, and he asked me to give the Sunday messages when he was away at conferences or on vacation. Unfortunately, he retired not long after and the position was filled by a young guitar-playing graduate from New Brunswick Seminary, a very apostate school. He did preach the gospel, but his form of charismatic worship was not for us.

We had similar experiences in two other local Presbyterian churches. One was Goodwill Presbyterian in Montgomery. Pastor Graham was a great old-time gospel preacher, as well as a warm and hospitable man. We really enjoyed that church and the Christian fellowship there. But our time there was cut short by the death of Rev. Graham. The pulpit was filled by another young guitar player whose messages were weak. At the same time the remaining congregation turned toward a Pentecostal form of worship unworthy of our Lord, so we left. Sad.

At that time two unusual things happened. First, Nelson Rockefeller, the governor of New York State proclaimed that he would make our local military airbase (which had just been handed over to the state) into the third major jet port in the New York Metropolitan area. In addition, he would commission the building of a high-speed commuter rail between the airport and New York City. The effect of these announcements was that property values in our county boomed. Land that we had purchased for less than $300 an acre was now selling for $3000 an acre. Farmers all over the county, and there were many (Orange County was one of the top five counties for milk production—dairy farms were everywhere) were delighted. With our acreage worth over ten times what we had paid for it, my partners saw dollar signs in their eyes. They wanted to sell the farm and quick. There was only one problem—we were raising a family there. After some serious negotiations, we agreed that they would cut out ten acres, the house, barns, pond, and creek and I would own that free and clear. They would get the farmland—252 acres now valued at $426,000. On paper, it looked like I had made a bad deal for myself. With the sale of 252 acres divided by three partners, my share would have been $142,000 a terrific sum for a ten-acre farmette. However, I would have gotten ten percent down and would have had to hold a mortgage for the balance. As it turned out, hanging on to the ten acres was the best decision I had ever made.

My partners sold 150 acres (the western property) to a New York City lawyer, and 102 acres to a Gigi chemical corporation executive. Everything was fine for about six months. I farmed the land that I had retained. In lieu of rent, I could get an agricultural tax exemption for keeping the land in ag production for the new owners. A fine proposition, but things were about to come crashing down. In 1974 Rockefeller became vice president under Gerald Ford, and Malcolm Wilson became governor of New York State. Soon after he assumed office, Wilson declared that there would be no jet port in Orange County. Instantly land values plummeted back to $300 per acre; investors who had put ten percent down on land and gave large mortgages to farmers defaulted, preferring to take the loss of their down payment than be saddled with paying farmers for property with so little value. Hundreds of farmers who had sold their property to these investors had taken their deposits and gone upstate, putting the deposit money down on new farms, depending on the mortgages on their old farms to pay for the mortgages they now owed. It was the biggest economic disaster our county had ever seen. Farmers had to take back ownership of their Orange County farms and pay non-agricultural taxes on that land, an expense these farmers could not afford. This forced many into bankruptcy. It was a terrible situation, but, thank God, we were free and clear of that situation.

The second phenomenon that occurred happened in the beef cattle industry. The problem began with the limited number of beef breeds in our country. Besides the specialty breeds of cattle—Brahma in the South and longhorns in Texas, there were only two breeds—Angus and Herefords. These cattle had been inbred for years, and consequently had become smaller, averaging only about 400 pounds of usable meat. The industry needed new blood to produce a bigger cow. There were numerous breeds available, but they were overseas. The USDA (United States Department of Agriculture) declared that farmers could not bring these cattle directly into the country because of a fear of hoof-and-mouth disease. Consequently, a new industry was born—the artificial insemination of beef cattle. This allowed the importation of breeds such as Charolais, Simmental, and other large breeds of cattle to be introduced to the United States.

These breeds would produce an additional 200 pounds or more of usable meat. However, you first had to inseminate a domestic cow with semen from these exotic breeds. This would give you a half-blood calf. The process would have to be done three more times until you reached a 15/16 offspring, which would be considered a purebred. The process would take over ten years to get a purebred calf. However, if you could transplant a purebred embryo into a recipient domestic cow, you could get a purebred calf in one year. The potential advantage was huge, so the industry of artificial insemination and embryo transplant of beef cattle took off.

As soon as I could, I formed a limited partnership company called Cattletec Farm Management Services. I began attending courses and clinics at Cornell University in animal nutrition, artificial insemination, and embryo transplant.

Once again I want to avoid going into all the details of all the clients I had at Cattletec. But I feel I must mention two of them. Tom Dexter, a wealthy man from New Jersey who had been the founder and owner of Dexter Press, was famous for the penny postcard and process of printing the full-color postcard in the 1930s. Tom owned a large cattle ranch in central Florida where he maintained a herd of 400 mixed-breed Angus-Hereford cows, and he was interested in breeding them to one of the exotic breeds for the potential of a larger herd. He was also interested in embryo transplants, but no one on the farm knew anything about the artificial breeding process.

So in the early spring of 1973, Charley, who was six months pregnant, Billy, Dan, and I headed off to Florida to set up his farm manager, Jim Pringle, in the artificial breeding business. Shortly after we arrived back home to the farm, our third son, Timothy, joined the family. (A side note—being a mother of three earned Charley a new name—Mom). After I met Jim and assessed the facility, Tom and I studied the range of cattle available for artificial breeding to improve his herd. Finally, he settled on the Chianina (KEY-a-NEE-nah) breed. This impressive cow from Italy stood six feet at the shoulders—the largest breed of cattle in the world. We could get the animal's semen locally, but embryos were available only from a single farm in England. So Tom, his wife Mildred, and I made plans to see the farm and make arrangements for a transplant procedure.

Tom had recently sold Dexter Press to Beatrice Foods, which

also owned General Mills. Beatrice made two offers, and under one Tom could have gotten $30 million in stock, but he settled for a second option—$10 million in cash. Tom put the $10 million in the bank and lived on the interest—about $500,000 a year. Now, this provided enough income for a man to live well, but Tom was the ultimate penny pincher. Perhaps it was because he had lived through the Great Depression. One would think that he and Mildred now were taking their first trip abroad that he would treat her to a first-class experience. No, not Tom. We flew in tourist class on the cheapest flight he could find. Hippies lined the aisles to use the lavatories; we could not talk between the aisles, and the plane smelled like a marijuana den. There was no prohibition against smoking on board at that time, plus we were over international waters. When we landed, I found things were no better. The flight was not the only sign of his excessive frugality. He rented the cheapest car he could find—it didn't even have a trunk. So, all of our luggage was piled in the rear seat with poor little Mildred. I drove unable to see the road behind us because of the mound of suitcases. And the hotel we stayed in was a flea-trap, and the food was horrendous. Finally, I had enough. I took Tom aside that afternoon and said, "Tom, how can you do this to Mildred? (They had been married for fifty years). If you spent one percent of what you get in interest alone each year, you could give Mildred the experience of her life and give her memories to last the rest of her life. Now, what memories will she have of this trip? Choking on smoke on the flight over, jammed in a shoebox of a car, staying in a hotel unfit for dogs and food that is its equal." Well, that did it. Did I get fired? No, no. We traded our car up for one with a trunk big enough to hold all of our luggage, searched out restaurants that served great food and stayed in four-star hotels. And when it was time to go home, they flew first class. I went tourist class, but that was

146

fine. Our time visiting the farm was highly profitable. Tom and I got to see the purebred Chianinas, and I knew they were something special—six feet tall and pure white. Seeing these beautiful animals and the English countryside again made the trip for me.

Bill with a 1 ½-year-old Chianina heifer, England, 1976

Black "host" mother nurses two white Chianina calves due to the innovation of embryo transplant, England, 1976

Tom and I became good friends, and we shared many other experiences in pursuit of farming success, but after my consulting time was complete, we parted ways. Just after my time with Tom, Mom gave birth to our fourth son, Stephen. The clan was growing, and it was great raising the boys on a farm.

At that time I met my biggest client—Bill Mulderig. He was a lawyer about my own age, and his business was tax shelters. His plans centered around buying farms in New York State and New England, both beef, and dairy, and selling small groups of cattle to investors at a premium price. These men could write the purchase price and the operational costs off their taxes. He wanted me to manage the farms where they were kept, hire the people, oversee the nutrition and health of the animals and make sure that all of the farms had the necessary equipment to operate efficiently. This also meant planning for the planting of field crops and doing financial statements for each farm. This was a massive job. So I got started. He bought three farms with 250 milking cows and two beef cattle farms with about 200 cows on them. I had many responsibilities working for Mulderig. With Dr. Gene Gill, I took care of the veterinarian needs of his trotting horse stable in Florida.

Mulderig called me in one day and said, "Now I want to buy several farms in Vermont." One of the properties was the Bushy Farm in Essex Junction near Burlington. He said that it had approximately 300 head of dairy cows and over 250 acres of good farmland. "I want you to go up," he said, "and analyze the cows, equipment, and operation so that I can make a proper offer to the owner."

I contacted two friends—Henry DeVries and Tom Ackuma—to agree to fly up with me to do an assessment. Henry had many years of experience in dairy farming and was an expert with large herds, and Tom was an equipment buff. I rented an airplane, and we all flew up to Burlington one early morning. Henry examined the cows, Tom checked the equipment, and I went over the finances. The results were mixed. Henry reported that a third of the cows were not bred. That meant that there would be no milk from them that year. A cow had to calve to produce milk so we could not expect income from them a third of the herd for at least a year. Tom's inventory of the equipment showed that half of the machines had to be replaced within the year. I found that the farm was running at a major loss. I put all of the information into a report and took it to Mulderig. To my surprise, he tossed the papers aside. "It doesn't matter," he said. "I bought the place yesterday."

"Why," I asked, "did we do all of this work? Why didn't you wait until I gave you the report? You could have bargained with the owner on all of the expense you will need to keep the farm going. You could have saved $200,000 or $300,000 off the asking price." But it was over. He bought the farm without my report, wasted all our time but would pay a bitter price later.

Bill Mulderig may have had poor business judgment, but he was a very generous man. In addition to the farms, he owned several condos in Stowe, Vermont, and he let our family use them at no cost for vacations. We hiked and biked, went on Alpine slides, played golf, and enjoyed great food at the local restaurants like the Shed and the Whip. We had wonderful family memories.

I was very sad to hear that Bill, because of his shoot-from-the-hip-ask-questions-later style, landed in legal trouble and he had to eventually sell all the farms.

I had many opportunities to talk with Bill about the gospel, most of them over a Heineken after work. Although I made some headway, he was Roman Catholic and steeped in the traditions of his faith. I missed working with him.

A close friend, from my college days at Nyack, Wayne Jamison, introduced me via tapes and books, to Dr. R.C. Sproul of Ligonier Valley Ministries. Sproul would change my life forever.

CHAPTER XIII

CAPTURED

What doest thou here, Elijah? The holy and the zealous grieve if they see we are a Christian ministering to his own ambition. We are only as strong as our commitment is perfect, unless we live wholly for God, our strength will suffer serious leakage, and our weakness will be the kind which degrades the believer till the ungodly scornfully ridicules.
—Charles Spurgeon

If I sinned, (and of course I have) it's because I loved creation too much. I really think only a farmer can truly appreciate what God has brought in His creation. I remember as a boy standing in a hay field with my hair whipping around. It made me think of the wind blowing over tall timothy and orchard grass, giving them the appearance of billowing ocean waves. I remembered watching Bill and Dan, Bill Decker's draft horses plod steadily over the fields, pulling hay into windrows with my dad's new dump rake, recently bought at a farm sale. Whether we forked the hay onto wagons as we did in '41 or baled it as we do now, the smell of the fresh cut hay is better than the finest perfume. And the labor of getting down in the dirt to remove rocks from a new field makes eating the sweet corn that would be planted there worth it.

Birthing 100 calves and watching them frolic in the joy of new life; drinking cold water from our hand-dug well; letting the condensation from the glass spill down your chest on a hot, dusty summer day; showing your prize heifer at the county fair, surrounded by the squealing of pigs, bucking of hens, and crowing of roosters, the bleating of lambs, and the baaing of sheep; cutting firewood to warm you in winter when you come in from chores; eating Mrs. Decker's raspberry rhubarb pie or Mom's turkey dinners; watching the sun go down behind the Shawangunks; huddling under the warm covers and listening to the Grand Ole Opry; sleeping until the sun barely cleared the horizon, and doing it all over again—what could be better than that? From the coral islands of the Caribbean to the magnificence of the Grand Canyon, from the Yosemite Mountains in the west to the crashing of waves at Schoodic Point in Maine, the Trinity outdid itself on this creation. I and the rest of humanity have screwed it up, but what a creation it is.

Ol' Bill Decker and his favorite workhorse, Dan.

A farmhand forking haylage into the blower
the old-fashioned way, 1943

One of my beloved Brown Swiss cows
and her two-month-old half-blood
Chianina calf at our farm, 1984

I know that the Apostle Paul told the Corinthian church, "Things which eye saw not, and ear heard not, and which entered not into the heart of man, Whatsoever things God prepared for them that love Him" (I Corinthians 2:9, ASV). However, this creation in its pristine form will be hard to beat. Oh, memories, memories—for some they draw up horrible or sorrowful visions of the past, for me they bring up wonderful experiences of years gone by. I fear to leave them behind.

I have to shake my head a little and get back to present-day reality. I wanted to continue my studies. However I still had 800 cows and five farms to take care of.

Two half-blood Brown Swiss Chianina calves at our farm in NY

This plus my own farm of thirty head and calves coming almost every day. In addition, I had three boys playing baseball in Pine Bush Little League, which was having difficulty finding coaches for the teams. So I volunteered to coach. At one point I was coaching three teams. Trying to schedule all of these activities, practices, and make all of their games was a nightmare, especially after driving all the way from Vermont every few days to make a game starting at six o'clock. I did not have much time to study, but I used my driving time to listen to tapes by R.C. Sproul and jot down notes. I also studied in the late evenings.

One problem with family activities developed at that time. During hot summer days, my boys' Little League friends invited them to their houses to go swimming in their pools. Mom and I observed that some of the families exhibited inappropriate behavior in front of the kids—smoking, drinking, and cursing. We didn't want the boys exposed to that style of life. Solution: build a pool.

Putting in a pool was a great idea, but there were problems—no flat land near our house was one, and the other was the average price quoted by dealers: $35,000, which included the excavation. So I decided to dig out the bank, make a flat surface, and build the pool myself. (I am including this story because it played a factor in a transformation I experienced later.) The pool I settled on was 18' x 38', eight feet at the deep end and four feet in the shallow end. I leveled the land and dug the hole for the pool myself with the help of my old backhoe and John Deere tractors. I bought the frame and liner wholesale for a total expense of $3000. Later, with the help of two friends, we completed the job. Total cost: $3500. We also tried to keep our kids in a private Christian school for the same reason we built the pool and to provide a Christian education.

I slowly continued my studies in the Gospels. Some verses began to haunt me. I couldn't get them out of my mind. In Luke 14:33, Jesus says, "Whoever does not forsake all that he has cannot be My disciple."

The Amplified Bible says, "So then, any of you who does not forsake (renounce, surrender claim to, give up, say goodbye to) all that he has cannot be My disciple," (Luke 14:33, AMP).

Also, Jesus said in Matthew 19:21, "If you would be perfect, go and sell what you have and give to the poor ... be My disciple" (AMP).

Jesus said further in Mark 8:34-35, "Then He called the crowd to Him along with His disciples and said: "Whoever wants to be My disciple must deny themselves and take up their cross and follow Me. For whoever wants to save their life will lose it, but whoever loses their life for me and for the gospel will save it" (NIV).

Jesus continued, in Matthew 16:24, "Then said Jesus unto His disciples, "If any man would come after me, let him deny himself, and take up his cross, and follow Me" (ASV).

The Apostle Paul reinforces this declaration of Jesus, "I beseech you therefore, brethren, by the mercies of God, to present your bodies a living sacrifice, holy, acceptable to God, which is your spiritual service," (Romans 12:1, ASV).

Wow! And I thought I was a disciple. Apparently not. Day after day, night after night His words kept going through my mind. "If you would be My disciple, sell what you have." They kept going around like a broken record.

The next morning, I got up early as I usually did before going to work or to Vermont to check on my herd. I would check every cow's udder to see if any mastitis was developing. I'd make the cows and their calves walk a little to make sure that none of them were lame or developing hoof problems. That morning I stood back in the barnyard and took in the beauty of my circumstances. I thought, "This herd and their calves are beautiful." The weather that brisk late summer morning was cool and magnificent. "What a blessing from God," I thought. I have a wife, four healthy tow-headed boys and a baby girl in the hangar on the way. I have a beautiful farm on a hill with a four-acre lake and the Dwaarkill River running through the property. I had a small flock of chickens, two sheep, a pig and her piglets, and a sizeable vegetable garden. I had John Deere tractors and a barn full of hay. I had a new swimming pool and a large farmhouse. And to top it all off, I had no mortgage and a good job that allowed me to set my own hours!

As I stood there that cool summer morning reviewing all of

the blessings that God had bestowed on me, a verse of Scripture jumped into my mind. "Or despisest thou the riches of His goodness and forbearance and longsuffering, not knowing that the goodness of God leadeth thee to repentance?" (Romans 2:4, ASV).

These words rattled in my hollow brain. "Goodness, riches, patience, forbearance, repentance." I dropped to my knees in that beautiful, smelly barnyard. It's hard to admit publicly, but tears were running down my face. How could I have been so blind and so selfish? I repented of this egocentric sin. I wanted to be a disciple; I would do whatever that would take!

In 1958 in the backseat of the admiral's car, God revealed Himself to me. After twenty years of His forbearance and longsuffering with me, almost to the day, August 1978, He captured me.

Well, I got off my knees, brushed the cow poo off my pants, went into the house and told Mom, "We cannot be fooling around with Christianity. We've got one foot in the world and one foot in Christ. If we are not all in, we are not in at all." She agreed.

So where to start? His words kept rattling in my head. "Sell what you have. Give to the poor." I started with that command. Previously, I had sold my boat, Aztec and Super Cub. Next, my cows. This was the hardest thing because I loved Brown Swiss cows, but they were an impediment to my new service to the Lord.

As the money started coming in, I began to look for the poor. Really there was no one destitute in our area. In Jesus's day there were beggars on every street, but in the USA, they were harder to find. So I looked overseas. At that time, the World Relief Commission needed help to relocate refugees from war-torn Southeast Asia, so I sent them a large chunk of money. A week later I got a call from WRC's president thanking me for the donation, but then he added, "I've got a large Laotian family of ten. They've been in an internment camp for eight years. We can't relocate them in the States because no one wants to take a family of that size. You have a farmhouse. Can you help us?"

I asked him to wait a moment, covered the mouthpiece of the phone and called my wife. I explained the situation, thinking that she would dampen the idea, but Mom answered, "Bring them on." Was she crazy?

I started thinking of all the challenges—use of water, overflowing septic system, food enough for seventeen. We only had two bathrooms and three bedrooms, there would be transportation problems (my station wagon only had six seats, although there was room in the back for a few others.) there would be doctors' and dentist bills, and money needed for clothes. But Mom said, "Do it—get them out of there."

So I removed my hand from the receiver and with fear and trembling said, "We will do it."

"Good," he said. "They will be at Kennedy Airport in about a month. We'll keep you posted."

Well, Jesus had commanded, "Sell all you have, give it to the poor... when you've done it to the least of these my brethren, you've done it unto Me." I felt like I was on the narrow road.

I had one month to get ready. One month to turn my basement, with pipes running all over it, into a bunkroom, and one month to make my attic into a bedroom.

Around a month later the plane came in bearing ten nervous Laotians with an odd assortment of clothes and bewildered looks on their faces. They had with them a number of bags containing traditional cooking paraphernalia and other personal items. As we stood in the waiting room, we attempted to sort them out— Kham Sing, the father, and his wife, Kham Pheng. From oldest to youngest were Vieng Xi and Vieng Kham, daughters, Khan Keo, son, daughters Lot Kham, Boun Then, Boun Mi and Hom, and the baby son Tet. The first problem was the limitation of language—the parents knew none, and the older girls knew very little. After retrieving their luggage, we herded them to our car for the ride home. After their long flight, they were very hungry, and we stopped at a fast food restaurant, named Carrolls in Newburgh. They seemed never to have seen a hamburger or French fries and were unsure as to how to eat them. Regardless of their awkwardness, they managed to run up a $75.00 bill. I thought, "Add to this our four boys and we are probably not going to be eating out much." We arrived home and settled the family in. With the arrival of morning, the challenges began. Some of the children had been born in the refugee camp and had no understanding of indoor bathrooms, or seen indoor lights or electric appliances. They had never taken a shower, and knives, forks, and plates were unfamiliar to them. Besides these difficulties, Tet was barely one year old and was used to nursing, even in public. After getting help from a missionary friend, we were able to explain to Khan Pheng that public exposure of breasts was not acceptable in the U.S. Her reaction surprised us. Through her daughter, she indicated that she needed iodine, which she proceeded to smear on her breasts. The next time Tet tried to nurse, he reacted to the bitter taste with a grimace and weaned himself in one afternoon.

Well, the wife and children proved to be wonderful. The father, however, had some issues that we didn't learn about until quite a bit later. With sixteen of us living in one house, the first month was a bit chaotic. I wondered what I had gotten myself into. I put a sign on my desk that helped remind myself why. "Sell what you have, give to the poor, take up your cross, and follow Me." A few months after the Laotians arrived, Mom gave birth to our fifth child, a daughter Kristen Kathleen Spanjer. Finally, a girl. Sooner than we could have thought, she was a blonde toddler, scooting around with her little dog, Nit Noy (Laotian for "small portion") and later on, in the providence of God, she would save my life.

I could go on and on about all of the incidents that we laughed and groaned about, but I will limit myself to two here. One of the pleasanter surprises we were to learn was that Kham Sing had been a gourmet cook for a French restaurant in Vientiane, Laos before he was forced to flee to Thailand. He truly was a superb cook. One day Mom brought home a large roasting chicken. Kham Sing took it to make dinner for all of us. He carefully stripped all of the meat off of every bone. Then he took half of the meat and put it in the refrigerator. The remaining meat he put in a large pot. He boiled the bones in another pot for several hours, then took them and dried them in the hot sun for the rest of the day. He took the water that the bones had boiled in, threw in some carrots, potatoes, celery, onions, parsley, and some seasoning. Then he deep fried the bones and fried the skin that he had removed earlier until it crackled. He steamed five pounds of sticky rice that we had purchased earlier on a trip to China-town, made gravy from the crackled skin and there we had it—a three-course dinner. The best chicken soup I have ever eaten, French-fried bones that rivaled the most delicious French-fried potatoes, chicken and gravy over the rice and cracklin' chips on the side. In addition, we had fresh bread that he had baked while the rest of the meal cooked. All sixteen of us left the table full and satisfied. And amazingly half of the chicken was still in the refrigerator. What U.S. housewife could match that!

One day Kham Sing came running to me crying, "Mr. Bill, Mr. Bill," and signaling that he wanted a spear and pointing to the Dwaarkill River. The only thing I had was a pitchfork, which he took and ran back to the river. He came back smiling with two large carp, one of which was the largest fish I had ever seen.

It was over thirty inches long, half as long as our ten-year-old son was tall. That was the way he had fished in Laos. Well, I was impressed with his fishing prowess, but how to cook them? I heard how it was to be done. Get a pine board and bake the fish on it with generous amounts of lemon and butter. Then throw away the fish and eat the board! The carp had NO flavor.

Billy Jr. holding pike Kham Sing speared in Dwaarkill River.

Another Friday, the family got word that a large group of Laotians were going to have a big picnic in Binghamton that Sunday. They were jumping all around me. "Can we go? Can we go?" Well, I had bought Mom a new Country Squire station wagon a few months before I had my barnyard experience. It was big enough to handle my gang of seven, but could it fit seventeen of us? Squeezing made no difference—everyone wanted to go. So here was the seating plan. Six in the front seat, with Mom holding Kristy on her lap, Kham Pheng with Tet on hers. Boun Then sat next to me and Kham Sing and three kids filled the back seat. That left seven kids on the platform in what we called the "way back." We were quite a load; in fact, the wagon bottomed out over bumps. I drove very carefully, and the trip took two and a half hours one way. They had a wonderful time talking to their countrymen in their language, and we attended a church service given in Lao. Afterward, the missionary who led the church spent some time with Kham Sing and Kham Pheng, listening to their concerns and answering their questions. She was able to share with us what they were thinking, and we left there feeling that we had a better understanding of our family. When it was time to head home, we packed back in the station wagon and headed down the highway. About halfway home, Vieng Xi tried to tell us that Boun Mi was not feeling well, but before we could pull over and get her out into the fresh air, the little girl threw up all over the back of the car. Everyone piled out while we cleaned up the best we could, and then, with all windows open, we took off once more. Finally, at about eleven p.m. we pulled into the driveway, safe at last, but the springs and shocks never recovered from the five hours of pounding.

Although we could recount pages of incidents and experiences, time here won't allow it. The family stayed with us for a little over a year. We really loved them and came to think of them as part of our family, our cultural differences required patience, and we found our budget stretched more often than we had expected, but God was faithful and always met our needs.

A few months after they arrived, we felt it was time that they become somewhat independent. I found Kham Sing a job as a cook in a high-end restaurant in the area, where he made over $500 a week take home. We opened a bank account in his name and got him a checkbook. In addition, we found a nice, fully furnished ranch house close to us, and paid three months' rent. We thought they were ready for independence, but it turned out that our expectations were a bit unrealistic. There were signs that they weren't as ready as we thought. One day Mom took Kham Sing shopping, and he quickly filled a huge shopping cart. At the checkout, Mom tried to show him how to write his first check. But when he realized that the money would come from his account (his balance was now about $3000), he refused. He was adamant, and kept repeating, "Sponsor pay, sponsor pay." We had two choices—put everything back, or pay for the groceries. So we paid. We began to feel a little unsure of their ability to cope with the new responsibilities, and so we checked in with them every day to make sure that they were alright. One December morning, I got a call from B & C, our heating oil company. The owner, Kenny Schliphack, said that he had gone over to their house a few days earlier to put in fuel oil and they refused to pay him C.O.D. I rushed over the next morning because that night the temperature had dropped dramatically. When I got there, I found Kham Pheng and the children huddled around the fireplace where a few small twigs were burning. The place was about fifteen degrees, a pipe had burst, and the basement was flooded. By the time I got the pipes fixed and the oil tank filled, it cost me over $1,500.

After trying unsuccessfully to get Kham Pheng to understand the situation, we called a meeting with the other Laotians living in the area. These men, who had small families, were all working two jobs and one of them worked three part-time jobs. They wanted to convince me to help him get on welfare. They couldn't understand why I was not getting this American benefit for him until I explained to them that the money the government would pay him was going to come out of their paychecks. All of a sudden the light dawned, and they changed their tune. From desiring him to get "free money" they began demanding that he take responsibility for his family with the money he was making.

We had learned in Binghamton that while the family was grateful for our care and concern, they desired to move into a settled Laotian community. After receiving correspondence from a cousin who had immigrated into a community in California, they expressed their desire to join them, and so we made arrangements for them to move. We shared the gospel with them during their stay here, and took them to church, took the children to VBS, but since only the two oldest girls knew much English, we could never be sure how much they understood. But we knew the time had come for them to move to a place where they would feel more comfortable. We bought them train tickets, piled everyone into the station wagon and headed down to New York City. I stopped by Battery Park first so that they could see the Statue of Liberty before they left. It was hard to say goodbye and Mom had tears in her eyes as she hugged them for the last time. As I watched them board the train, I remembered again the words of Jesus—"Sell what you have, give to the poor, take up your cross, and follow Me."

All to Jesus I surrender, Lord, I give myself to Thee.
Fill me with Thy love and power, Let Thy blessing
fall on me—
I surrender all; I surrender all.
All to Thee my blessed Savior, I surrender all.
—Judson W. Van DeVenter

Spanjer family together with Laotian family, 1980

CHAPTER XIV

FOLLOW ME—TO THE INNER CITY

Now, the word of Jehovah came unto Jonah the son of Amittai, saying, Arise, go to Ninevah, that great city, and cry against it; for their wickedness is come up before me. But Jonah rose up to flee to Tarshish from the presence of Jehovah; and he went down to Joppa, and he found a ship going to Tarshish (present-day Spain)" (Jonah 1:1-3, ASV).

One thing you can bet the farm on, country farm boys don't like city folks—they don't like their attitudes, dialect, or traffic congestion. They may be nice people when you get to know them, but country boys don't like concrete; they like dirt. All we want are peaceful, lightless nights, and calm days without sirens, screeching tires, and angry voices. We want the quiet of birds calling, the occasional sound of a bullfrog or a peeper, or a tractor putt-putting in a distant field. Being able to watch your neighbors through binoculars means they're too close. The farm where I grew up on and the one I now own, you can look to any point of the compass and see only fields, meadows and trees. The farm boy philosophy was good enough for me.

Until this chapter in my life, I had only been in New York City four times. The first time was when my mother took me to see the *Normandy* in 1944—a giant troop ship that was sabotaged in 1943 and it was left lying on its side in New York Harbor. We then went to see the Empire State Building, the tallest building in the world at that time. I can remember standing on the observation deck and looking at the vast city beneath me and asking my mom, "Do people really live here?"

My second visit was when my mother and I came back from Germany. That visit lasted only long enough for us to get out over the George Washington Bridge. The third time came about because I had a great desire to see the Brooklyn Dodgers play a home game at Ebbets Field in the spring of 1953. I couldn't get even one of my baseball buddies to go with me—they said they didn't want to go through the city. The fourth time was when I took the Laotians to the train. That is it—the sum total. And in those days, that was quite enough for me.

There is an old saying among missionaries. "Don't tell the Lord where you would prefer not to go because that is where you will end up."

I had never wanted to go to New York City, let alone the inner city, but that's where I was headed.

About a week before the Laotians left for Los Angeles, I got a call from an old college friend, Wayne Jamison. He and his wife, Jane, were my best friends in college days. Wayne had gone from Nyack to Trinity Seminary. He had been ordained and served in the Army for a stint as a chaplain in Viet Nam. After his return, he and his family, which now included three children, settled in Stuyvesant Town on the Lower East Side of Manhattan where Wayne wanted to plant a church. He asked me if I could bring the family down to a space he had rented for church services on Sundays because at that point he had no congregation yet in New York City.

Although I was still a confirmed country boy with an aversion to big cities, I thought that going to help a church start up was a reason to go. So all seven of us packed up the next Sunday and headed down to the Lower East Side.

Now the back of our station wagon looked like a sports locker, equipment for every season. Pails of baseballs, gloves, and a baseball bat, a soccer ball, and a football. The reason? On family trips, at fuel stops, we always took time to participate in that season's activities, so after attending Wayne's church service (we were the only ones there), on our way up Fifth Avenue, we noticed Central Park. I thought, that would be a good place to get some exercise before making the two-hour trip north. So we parked, found a big opening, tossed the football around while Mom and Kristy bathed in the afternoon sun.

Soon two young boys came over and asked if they could join us, and before long there were about twenty boys wanting to play. Well, we had plenty of players, so we split up into two teams and spent the next hour in a spirited game of touch football. When all of us were pooped out, I gathered the boys by some large rocks nearby and explained the basic gospel to them. When I closed in prayer, some of the kids asked, "Could you come back next Sunday?" Now I had two reasons to want to go to New York City on Sundays.

The next Sunday that we went down to Wayne's church, where there was the beginning of a small congregation, we again stopped at Central Park. There, to our surprise, we found a small crowd of about thirty kids looking to get the game started. There were almost too many to break up into teams with my kids there also. We did play for a while and then I did what I had done the first week, by the rocks. This time, however, I took some of the older kids aside and talked to them separately. I found out that most of them were from East Harlem, up around 116th Street, and they asked if the next time I came down, I would come to their park.

A few weeks later I went over to Marcus Garvey Park, which ran from 120th to 125th Streets. I noticed that a good number of the boys were the same ones I had met my last time down. And now I knew some of their names—Jorge Camacho, Neal West, Angel Rivera, Charley Perez. With them, there were about twenty other boys. They wanted me to come down every week to meet with them—they did not know that I was a country boy who hated the "concrete jungle." However, I could see that they were a needy group, and I felt that they needed a cause or a mission. And they were very receptive to the gospel, so I agreed. But we didn't have a place to meet, so the next time I came down we held a Bible study right in the park.

Now, in the providence of God, to show how He works everything out, a local pastor, Rev. Ezra Williams and his congregation had recently purchased P.S. 120, an abandoned middle school—a huge, four-story, 300-foot long granite building right across the street from Marcus Garvey Park. One day I bumped into him on the street and he asked, with good humor, "What are you whities doing here?" I told him our story and the problem we were having with finding a meeting place. He listened thoughtfully and then said, "I'll give you a class room in the school building that you can use whenever you want." I could hardly believe what I was hearing. Now we had a place to meet, and the boys moved right in. We moved desks and chairs into the room, and the boys began to call themselves a team.

When I drove home that night and began to think over the way things had worked out, I realized that I had gotten myself into a big project. The kids couldn't just meet—they had to have a purpose. So Mom and I formed a non-profit 501(c)3 company. I named it Affirmative Evangelism Fellowship, which simply meant "doing positive things for people to call them to God and Christ." Then, with the kids in mind, I set out to form a structured program that I thought would get them on a course to spiritual and personal success.

First, after getting to know these kids personally and visiting their homes and apartments, I discovered a number of disturbing facts. First, the majority of these inner-city kids had no kitchen tables in their apartments. There were small tables, of course, but they were piled up with papers and family items. It became apparent that they had no sit-down family meals where activities of the day would be discussed, where parent/child accountability and encouragement would be expressed. I compared this to my childhood situation. We ate as a family at six o'clock every night. My dad would ask every member of the family, including my stepmother, what he or she did that day, and what important thing was learned. And he set the tone by relating what had happened in his day. When we all concluded our narratives, Dad would say to each of us, "Do it better tomorrow." Besides the encouragement we received from this admonition, the three of us kids knew doing better, including raising the grades on our report cards, could result in an increase in allowance. Of course, the opposite was true—a backsliding would lead to a decrease. Now I could see that this natural, family-centered accountability and support were things my city kids never experienced.

One thing that I noticed was there was no night time in the inner city. Lights seem to illuminate every corner of Manhattan, so kids can hang out shooting hoops or merely socializing into the late night or early morning hours. Because of a lack of parental accountability, there was no concept of time—when you have to be here or there. Staying out on the park courts until two in the morning meant these kids couldn't get up for school in the morning. So they would come to school at ten o'clock or noon, thus they would fail a good number of their classes. One would expect that they would have to repeat these classes, but principals in these schools, faced with the problems that large numbers of students repeating would create, plus an unwillingness to make the school's drop-out statistics look bad, just pass them and ultimately graduate them. There is no accountability, civil or personal, to God or society. Not seeing themselves as created in God's image and responsible to carry out His character in their lives, and not inspired to be self-supportive, contributing citizens of their communities, the majority of these inner-city kids are led down the one-way street of moral, ethical and social decay, and ultimately a total lack of character. This affects the girls by conditioning them in a cycle of government dependence. When Mom had conversations with the girls, they would admit that their mothers would encourage them to become pregnant so they could get social services (i.e. food stamps, welfare, Medicaid, housing assistance, etc.) This would be their future—a successful future their parent would proclaim.

The boys fare no better. They came out of their teen years with no real education; they could only get menial labor jobs at best. Their situations left them open to the culture of drugs and petty crime, to which many, for reasons of survival, succumbed. They are caught in a vicious cycle of dependence. It produced children with no fathers, kitchens with no family dinners, children with no solid education, no inspiration, no salvation, and ultimately no real hope of genuine success in their futures.

I felt discouraged. What could I tell them; what could I do to elevate them from this cycle of failure? I discovered that most of the kids in our program were from the description mentioned above, or had a single mom who wanted to help them get out of this vicious cycle.

As a result, I started weekly team meetings with the kids. I had an hour and a half with them every Wednesday night. I thought first the team needed structure, so I broke up the meetings up into three parts. First I knew that they had to get right with God, so I began the meetings by sharing the gospel. Each one of them was a sinner (they heartily agreed); their sins would lead to them being judged by God and ultimately doomed to eternal punishment. I explained that Jesus Christ thought they were too valuable for such a destiny, and paid their debt for their sins on the cross, now offering them eternal life in return for their repentance and faith in Him.

The next second half hour we discussed the theology of Christian living. I had a teaching session with the kids using Scripture to show them how to live in society, being made in the image of God, and the responsibility of bearing the *Imago Dei*. The third half hour was devoted to loving our fellow man, those others in our community who the Bible requires us to love, our neighbors. With that goal, the team would plan a human need project that would be done the following week. I called these Matthew 25 Projects, from passage in which Jesus told his disciples, "For I was hungry and ye gave Me to eat; I was thirsty and ye gave Me drink; I was a stranger, and ye took Me in; Naked, and ye clothed Me; I was sick and ye visited Me; I was in prison, and ye came unto Me... Inasmuch as ye did it unto one of these My brethren, even these least, ye did it unto Me," (Matthew 25:35-36, 40, ASV).

The kids were creative and thought up many projects to meet the needs they saw all around them. Shopping for shut-ins and cleaning some of the local streets were two of the more successful projects they put in to action.

We then closed the meeting with prayer and returned to our homes. I found myself eagerly anticipating the next week's meeting.

When I set up the teams, I made regular church attendance a requirement, and recommended, for the kids in the East Harlem area, Ezra Williams's church, Bethel Gospel Assembly. Bethel was not a "blended" church—they were all in for the gospel and had a strong ministry to their local community. They ran a social service ministry that provided professional counseling to the poor and fed 1,500 to 2,000 people annually. They had nineteen small discipleship groups from youth groups to senior citizen groups as well as groups that ran street evangelism and prison ministries, among others. They supported missionaries in over twenty countries around the world and founded a Christian school in East Africa.

Bethel's growth and influence for the Lord were directly apportioned to the people's sacrifice to the lost with the gospel. This was exactly the influence I wanted my Conquest kids to be exposed to.

Now the kids had a purpose and a cause to bring them together. I threw in a plum. I would take the whole team up to my farm for one weekend every quarter for a team retreat. I called this youth ministry, "Youth Conquest with Christ"—noting that you have to fight to be a Christian in a culture that wants you to submit its norms.

It happened that at this same time, the spring of '81 I had three sons in Little League. Our League had three levels: Mini-minors (ages seven and eight), Minor A (ages eight and nine) and Majors (ages ten, eleven, and twelve) and not enough adults to help. Les Sheeley, the president of the League, called me and said he didn't have enough coaches for a mini-minor and a minor league team, which would leave about thirty boys who would be unable to play that year. Now at that time, I was coach of the Dodgers, a major league team, but I said, "Les, I'll coach the other two teams as well." I did not know what I was thinking! I still had four farms in Vermont to manage for Bill Mulderig. That meant getting up a four in the morning, driving five hours to the first farm and getting there about ten a.m. Then spending an hour at each farm and driving another five hours back to the town park, spending an hour with each team and getting home at nine for dinner. I was still trying to disperse my herd of cattle, and now I took on the inner-city Conquest team. My schedule was full, but these were great days.

That's when I got the name Coach. I had about thirty kids coming up to me—"Mr. Spanjer, can I go call my mom?" or "Mr. Spanjer, I got to go to the bathroom."

So enough with the Mr. Spanjer routine. "Just call me Coach." My kids were there also, and so it was, "Mom and Coach" for thirty-seven years and counting.

Meanwhile, the Conquest team was getting bigger and ready to come upstate for their first quarterly retreat. We were planning a one-week summer program for Conquest in August. I talked it over with Mom. "Where are we going to sleep twenty-five inner-city kids? And where can I assemble them?" We could take five to ten. I asked a few Christian friends who had a heart for evangelism and inner-city kids, Ron Bonagura, Roger Christine and Dan Brown, and they agreed. I cleared out space in our barn for classes and meetings, and we were set to go.

Youth Conquest on the quarterly weekend,
taking classes in my farm shop

Now, what about transportation? My first thought was the train. Metro-North stopped at 125th Street on its way to Beacon, a mere twenty minutes from the farm. But it was too expensive—$16 round trip per kid! Total for twenty-five kids, $400! Still, it seemed that we had no alternative. Until the problem was solved when I bought an old forty-passenger school bus to bring the Conquest kids up and back for the summer program.

I arranged the weekend like this: the kids would arrive by train on Friday night. One of my most capable team members, Jorge Camacho, would organize them in the city. Our host parents would pick them up at the train station and take them home. The next morning they would come to the farm at eight a.m. and begin the day with calisthenics. The first class, which was basic theology, would start at nine o'clock and last for an hour and a half. All team members were required to take notes and were provided with a Bible.

After a break, the second class, called Principles for Christian Living, began at eleven. After each class, short tests were given, and rewards were given for high scores. (Rewards were foreign concepts to them). At the midday break, Mom and Karin Bonagura and Judy Christine, Ron and Roger's wives, fed us lunch, and then it was time for competitive activities (a five-mile run, basketball games, baseball, etc.), and then at five o'clock they were picked up and taken back to their host homes. At their host homes they ate dinner with the families, and on Sunday they attended church with the host. On Sunday evening they came back to the farm for a devotional in my living room, and then back to the train at five. Then I would prepare for the next Wednesday meeting.

The kids' reactions to their time in the country were interesting. One said, "It was so quiet at night that I couldn't sleep," and another admitted that he had never eaten with his family except at a restaurant. Some said that they had never gone to church before that week. Ron and Roger were very excited about the kids and the program and expressed an interest in helping. Shortly after the first program, they each volunteered to take a Wednesday a month to lead the Conquest team meeting at Bethel Gospel Church.

"Arise, go to ... that great city, and cry against it; for their wickedness is come up before me" (Jonah 1:2, ASV). Spain or Nineveh? I chose Nineveh—I did not want to get swallowed by a fish.

CHAPTER XV

VALUE OF THE GOAL

The kingdom of heaven is like unto a treasure hidden in the field; which a man found, and hid; and in his joy he goeth and selleth all that he hath, and buyeth that field (Matthew 13:44, ASV).

God sets the bar very low for personal salvation. Believe, repent, and be saved. The Holy Spirit pushes people over the bar by the thousands every day. To become a disciple of Christ, however, is totally another issue: here the bar is extremely high. "Sell what you have, give to the poor, take up your cross (be crucified) and follow Me." Now that's a high bar to get over. But if you're committed to run the obstacle course, you've got to get over it.

Around this time Mom told me that an associate evangelist from the Billy Graham Association was going to speak at a local church that week. Having volunteered for the Graham Association in college, I wanted to go hear him. Ralph Bell was speaking on "The Committed Christian." In part of his message he said, "To be committed to Christ you must give Him your all, everything."

That, I thought, that's good preaching. Then he added, "When you have given Christ your money, your car, your house, your business, family, and life, God seeing that you are willing to do thus, gives all back to you." I was shocked! I could feel Mom pulling on my sleeve. I wanted to stand up and shout, "When you give everything to God and turn over all your assets to Him—He never ever gives it back to you! He keeps it forever and ever! What He does do is let you manage what are now His assets for Him. Now you are a manager in His vineyard, a manager of His property. You now own nothing. Christ wants everything you have, 100%. Now He gives you back only what you need to live and serve Him." The farmer found a box (the gospel) in a field with a treasure in it (Jesus Christ), and he sold all that he had and bought that valuable field to get that treasure. That is "sold out"; that is a crucified man—now a disciple.

The word about our inner-city ministry reached a mission-centered church led by Pastor Steve Offringa, who introduced me to a young man, Dan Narvaez, who wanted to help with our Conquest program. Dan, in turn, introduced me to Lily and Caesar Tariche from Union City, New Jersey, and through them I met Jerry Jones. They all wanted to have AEF Conquest team in their areas and to be leaders of other teams.

So now we had three teams and over sixty members, and my leaders wanted to start more. Mom and I had a long talk. We knew from our experience with the Laotians and the inner-city kids that we wanted to work with a youth ministry. These kids needed the gospel. They needed structure in their lives, good family role models, and a broader view as to their vocational options. But how could we handle them on our little farm? I thought that if we could sell our ten-acre farm and raise some other money and take out a small mortgage, we could perhaps buy an older camp property. Remember that Jesus said, "Sell what you have," so I talked to a realtor friend. He told me that he would be glad to list the property for us, but we were facing a down real estate market. He added that there were just too many places for sale in our area because of the Malcolm Wilson fiasco.

Then I looked up camps that were for sale. Most properties

that were in our price range needed substantial repairs—they were worn out. Two or three weeks went by. I was staring out of my home office window late one afternoon at the one flat acre that we owned, mulling over the dilemma I was facing—too many kids and not enough facility. A voice (I don't know if it was audible or simply in my mind) said, "Don't give Me what you hope to have; give Me what you have." Wow! Could I build a camp on my own property? I only had one flat building acre, and it was a narrow acre. I got out a piece of graph paper and started drawing. I designed a pole building, 50' by 100', with a foyer and two offices in the front portion of the building, and four classrooms behind these, a fellowship hall, 33'x50', and in the back left, boys' and girls' bathrooms. In the center, I designed a kitchen, 12'x15', and on the right rear, a small library. I figured out a rough cost for materials at about $80,000. I had $40,000 in the bank left over from my sales of cattle, equipment, and planes—enough to get started. So I did it myself with the help of a carpenter friend named Sal Napolitano to save money.

Conquest building under construction

Well, we held our quarterly Conquest meeting and summer program in that unfinished building until the early spring of 1986. During the summer programs, I changed the schedule a little. We still had early morning P.E., followed by a class in theology and then one in principles of Christian living, but in the afternoon I brought in Christian laymen to teach their vocations. We had classes in carpentry, excavation (all the kids got to drive the bulldozer and backhoe, as well the tractors) and I taught aviation. I gave four days of ground school and then, on Friday, took the team members to the airport and gave each a half-hour instructional flight, with a personal logbook signed by me certifying their flight time. The idea behind this vocational program was to expose these kids to vocational and professional experiences beyond their limited cultural norms and broaden the scope and vision of the opportunities of their lives. This, I believed, with a renewed relationship with God because of their faith in Jesus Christ, would be the inspiration to break

(clockwise from top left) Neal West on 7600 Ford, bulldozing during a Conquest weekend, Charlie Perez taking flying a lesson, Girls Team 105 showing off Bibles and bags, George Comacho doing morning calisthenics

the cycle of deception and dependence on the state created by the inner-city lifestyle. We began seeing good progress in their lives with both Christ and their culture.

Being a teacher, Mom liked to talk with the kids about their activities in school. She discovered that most of them were failing a number of their subjects, mainly for the reasons mentioned earlier. We realized that what these kids really needed was structure in their lives and a Christian education. The next day Roger Christine, one of my board members said, "Why don't we open a Christian high school? There isn't one anywhere around here."

"But," I said, "who's going to want to come to school on a dirt road in the woods, in a little 50'x100' building that looks like a barn." That night I thought seriously about Roger's words. I still needed $40,000 to $50,000 to complete the initial plans for the building. Now, on top of that expense, we would need desks, blackboards, teachers, curricula, and textbooks. And what about sports? High school athletic programs require prepared fields, a gym, tracks, and equipment. And we only had one building on a single acre. There was another potential problem—could city kids and country kids get along? What problems might such a situation create? I couldn't talk to others about it; no one local had ever tried it before. All this made the idea seem overwhelming to me. So I decided to take things in priorities. All of the things needed to begin and run a high school were possible to secure, including getting the building ready. Everything was possible. All I needed was money! That would be problem enough, but getting enough flat ground to run a credible physical education and sports program was my top priority. Would the owner next door sell a portion of his property, and if so, what would the price be? If the land was not available, I wouldn't be able to go ahead with the plan. I didn't want to run an unrespectable and embarrassing high school program. I wanted to give kids a balanced education, one equal to what a public school could offer, with a disciplined environment and a true spiritual emphasis, or I wouldn't run one at all. I would be content to continue our successful Conquest program as it was.

The next morning I got right to work researching the current landowner. And I discovered that the land was for sale. The owner had a mortgage for 150 acres with the Federal Land Bank for $180,000. I asked the banker if the bank would be willing to sell me a small portion of land that lay adjacent to my property, and he said no. The land could not be subdivided—it was all or nothing. Well, I thought, I started the flight school with over $200,000 in debt, and maybe I could do it again.

Public schools at that time had very negative environments with bullying, drugs, and fights rampant. Moreover, the Bible and prayer had been thrown out. Maybe, I thought, this is the time that church and Christian parents might consider investing in a Christian school. So I set out on a mission to talk to all of the church pastors in our area. I began with the pastor of a Pentecostal church in New Paltz and worked my way down two counties to Warwick Baptist Church, which already had a K-8 program. I thought we were able to offer a great opportunity for their graduating eighth graders to continue their Christian education. In all, I visited about twelve church pastors within a reasonable busing distance. They all said, No! Even after meeting with their elders. "There are no mission funds available for your project," they responded. Undaunted by these rejections, Roger and I set our sights on visiting the three K-8 Christian schools in our area, one of which Roger had served as principal. We felt that these schools would have a vested interest in what we were trying to do and give their graduates an opportunity to further their Christian education. However, they also said no. In fact, two of the facilities I had visited said that not only would they not give us funds, but they would oppose what we were attempting to do. One actually aggressively attacked us by trying to discredit me personally. The reasons we were given ranged from, "You are a para-church organization, and we do not approve of such groups," to "You have no credible board." I was becoming discouraged. What was I doing wrong? I knew that kids needed this program in an ever-more secularly progressive world. Why did I not get one church to come on board and agree, "We think your vision for our community is a positive thing?" Why did not one church say, "This would be a good home mission to support"?

I decided to first go back to by bank and then to a meeting with my directors. My banker said they would consider a mortgage for the property if all of my directors would sign the mortgage. So I called a meeting with my board at that time—Dr. Gene Gill, Lawrence Marci, Roger Christine, Ron Bonagura, and myself. I gave a report on my findings and what our banker had suggested. Marci said that the project was too risky, with no certainty that the community would support it and he stated, "I'm out." Gill said he didn't think the school was a wise idea—too risky. Ron and Roger liked the idea but felt that the idea did present a big risk.

I gave a final pitch. "Our city kids and our local kids need this program. We have the opportunity to change their lives forever. Let's do it for the Lord." Later that week Lawrence and Gene resigned from the board. Ron and Roger stayed on board, but they were just working guys like me and didn't really have extra resources to risk.

The bankers had said, "If all of your directors agree, we will consider it." I was shot down.

That week I moped around. There was a mountain of things against the plan—money to complete the building, housing for the inner-city kids, money to get us operational, teachers, curricula, transportation for local kids and the land. The odds against the project were high. I felt like the guys in the Book of Judges. Like Shamgar who fought off 300 enemy combatants with an ox goad, like Barak facing 500 chariots of iron or Gideon facing 10,000 men with a force of only 300. The odds were high for failure. The risk of proceeding must have overwhelmed them. Then I remembered Pop Suplee's one liner—"What side of the BUT are you on? Do you have the Lord BUT there is all this opposition against you—or you have all of this opposition against you, BUT you have the Lord?"

I was reading an article by Dr. Ralph Winter from the World Mission Center in Pasadena, California. His quote has stayed in my mind since the first time I read it: Risks should not be evaluated in terms of the possibility of success but rather in terms of the value of the goal.

I went to bed that night with those words going round and round in my mind, "value of the goal, value of the goal." That night God gave me a plan. Early the next morning I rushed down to the bank. I caught the banker just going in the door. Out of breath, I said, "I've got an idea!"

CHAPTER XVI

THE BLENDED CHURCH

So send I you to labor unrewarded. So send I you by grace made strong to triumph over hosts of hell, darkness and sin, My name to bear and in that Name to conquer. So send I you to talk to souls in bondage the words of truth that sets the captive free, to break the bonds of sin, to loose death's fatal grip, so send I you to bring the lost to Me.—Margaret Clarkson (Based on John 20:21)

I debated long and hard whether or not to include this chapter in this book. I don't want to paint with a wide brush. Not everything is within my experience. I want to remind the reader again that what is written here has been my own personal experience. The conclusions that I have reached and the truths that I have discovered are from my own observation, experiences, and studies. I don't claim to be a scholar or an intellectual, just a simple disciple trying to make sense of how the church carries out its mission as mandated by our Lord.

I once told my staff at a meeting and my children at a family get-together that I know that I have been a pain in the ass to almost everyone. By pain, I mean the face that holds another person accountable is an ugly face. Except for my father, Lawrence Yetter, and the Marine Corps, I have been a boss for all of my life. Holding people accountable is what I do; family, staff, students, and suppliers need to be accountable to the high standards of God, the claims of Jesus Christ, ethics, and morality. No matter how I demand this, whether politely, or with reasoning, or with persuasion, most all take it resentfully. This is why I am a pain in the ass to almost everybody. Consequently other than those mentioned above, I've gotten out of the accountability business. This chapter is an illustration of my conclusion.

The story begins in the summer of '61. It was my first summer home from college. I came north that summer to my old stomping grounds because I had friends there. It was cooler than Florida, and my home church was there. Don Castner, an elder in my church and a close friend, and his wife, Eleanor, gave me a room in their large Victorian home. Carl Luthman, my pastor, and mentor at that time, made an announcement in church the next Sunday that Bill Spanjer was home from college and needed summer work. Well, after the service, several people came up to me with job offers.

One was a fellow named John Dodd. He said that he just signed a contract to build a house for someone and needed a helper. Well, I wanted some outside work, so I agreed. The next morning John dug around in his wooded toolbox and found me a hammer and nail apron. I was ready to work. The person John worked for was Lou Vanderplate. He was a character right out of a Hemingway novel. I could write a whole chapter on his adventures and antics. One I will describe here because it will give my readers some background for the point of the story. Lou lived on the top of a large hill, in a small home with his wife and children; there was a long field on his property where he built a building that housed a Christian radio station. There he played Christian music, teachings, and basically spread the gospel in our community.

Vanderplate never did anything in conventional ways. He wanted to build a house—no problem. Buy a sawmill, move it onto the property, cut down trees, saw them into planks, and build a house! I was told Lou wanted to learn to fly a plane. No need to take flying lessons—just buy a plane and teach yourself! He bought a J-3 Cub, read some books on flying. He taxied his plane around the field next to his house and one day pushed the throttle forward and took off! I am told that he ground looped the Cub on his first landing, but no problem. He patched it up and took off again! Now, years later I knew something about flight instruction, having thousands of hours at it, and how complicated teaching a student to fly really is, but that was crazy Lou Vanderplate.

One morning when John and I showed up to work, we noticed a large school bus parked in front of the house we were building. John asked Lou what the bus was about. Lou said that he had bought an old abandoned church down the road. He gave us a week to fix it up. It was a great old church, built around 1865. We fixed the doors and patched the roof. After about a week, we returned to the house project. John asked Lou, "What's the school bus for?" Lou turned to me and said, "Spanjer, I want you to drive this bus to five proscribed stops in two local towns every Sunday. Open the door at each stop, wait five minutes, and then drive to the next stop. Then bring the bus back to the church. After the service and coffee hour, repeat the run." So the next Sunday Lou had painted, professionally, a large sign on both sides of the bus—"Church bus—pick-ups 9 AM, drop offs 12:30 PM." He had done a lot of advanced prep. Announcements on his radio station, flyers he and his wife handed out in each town and talks he gave at different organizations in the towns. So I began the run. I stopped at the proscribed stops, opened the door, waited five minutes, and moved on to the next stop. I repeated that for five stops. No one got on. I drove an empty bus back to the church where I sat with John, his wife and their two children and Lou's two children while Lou's wife played the piano and Lou preached a gospel message to us. I repeated the run after church, stopping at each stop, opening the door, and moving on to the next stop.

I had no passengers for the next three Sundays. On the fourth Sunday, I saw some women and children standing where I normally stopped. I asked myself, "What are they doing there?" So I pulled up a little further beyond them not to embarrass them with my big bus. I opened the door, and they came over. One of the women asked, "Is this the church bus?"

I answered, "Yes, ma'am." They got on, and I drove to the next stop. There I found one shabbily dressed man waiting. And he got on. We all went to the church, and now there were nineteen of us in the service.

Well, over the next few weekends I drove an almost-full bus to the church. It was great! By the end of the next month, with drive-ins and my bus loaded, we almost had a full church. Lou Vanderplate may have been crazy, but he was crazy like a fox. I was very impressed. And the abandoned church had come to life again. I learned a lot from that episode.

Vanderplate invested a lot of money fixing up the church and buying a school bus. He invested time in visiting the communities and suffered delays on building his house. He was laughed at by some, and some of those who laughed were Christians by the way, for having me drive an empty school bus week after week, but it paid big dividends in the end. "Audacity, audacity, audacity!" John Dodd took over my bus run, and I headed back to college to start my second year at CBC.

I am telling this story now because there is a point I'd like to make later in this chapter. I have become convinced over the years that American Christian churches have become "blended." If individual Christians are blended, the church must be blended also. By blended I mean that all Christians fall into one of three categories. They either have both feet in the bucket labeled "status quo" or one foot in the status quo bucket and one foot in the bucket labeled "crucified" or both feet in the "crucified" bucket. There are no other choices. Status quo Christians, although not admitting it, won't let go of their financial security, their present lifestyle, or their fear of risk. They are safe! Crucified Christians, on the other hand, are all in—bank accounts, lifestyle change, and a willingness to risk all for the gospel. They trust Christ for their survival no matter how bleak the situation gets. The Christians that have one foot in each bucket are called "blended Christians," and the churches they attend are blended churches. Their members have one foot in the status quo bucket and think one foot is in the crucified bucket. Their position "blends" from one to the other and consequently they fool themselves about the reality of discipleship. Everywhere I drive I see churches and steeples that are monuments to the status quo. A crucified church may not be a pretty church; it may not have the fanciest organ or even an organ at all. It may not have a large beautiful building situated on acres of property. It may not have the best heating system, and air conditioning would be beyond its budget. But what it would have is a conductive gospel energy, a mission outreach, both foreign and at home. I was talking once with a friend at my church about witnessing to the community. He said, "My neighbors see me going to church every Sunday at nine thirty a.m." He continued, "My church is located on a big hill where everyone can see it. That's my witness."

I thought that's fine and good, but that is a "static" witness; it's just glows—"Look at me, I am the church." Glowing is not going. I said our church needs conductive energy that accomplishes something. Only a crucified church will have the energy and vision to be conductive. It is conductive in the sense that it is not only accomplishing the ministry to its congregants (preaching, teaching Sunday school, administering the sacraments, counseling, etc.) but accomplishing the mission Jesus Christ gave to the disciples—"Go take this gospel out even to the uttermost." The purpose of Sunday church is communal worship. The heart of that worship is the desire to produce worship in others—that's called missions.

Static churches say, "Oh, we send some of our budget to the denomination and pray and let a few others carry our out responsibilities vicariously." These churches will even permit these missionaries to come into their churches and let them say a few words about their hardships and accomplishments during Sunday school or evening service. How gracious!

But our Lord says, "As the Father hath sent Me, even so send I you" (John 20:21, ASV). Note: this is a personal command, not a corporate or collective one. It is to you and me personally. Are we status quo or crucified, static or conductive? By his new birth, every Christian is a missionary. Do we put ourselves at risk for the gospel or do we play it safe? I am not judging individuals here. Maybe some, and I know of some that have both their feet planted firmly in the crucified bucket! Some are private, even secretive about their crucifixion. Jesus warns us of improper judgment—Get the log out of your own eye before trying to remove the speck out of your neighbor's eye (Matthew 7:5). However, Jesus also said, You will know THEM by their fruits (Matthew 7:16, 20). Notice it says "them" not necessarily individuals. So we do not judge individuals necessarily on this subject because we don't know the heart of each person in our congregations or what they do in secret. However, using reverse reasoning, we can judge "them" as a group if the church is "blended." One leads to the other. The conclusion, many of the congregants must also be blended.

Take my church for instance: it has totally correct theology. Down to the chapter and verse. Luther, Calvin, the best creeds, and confessions. The pastor is devoted, well-educated, compassionate, and diligent. His sermons are challenging and expository, and he always brings out the real meaning of the text. The people in our church are wonderful, very giving, and a praying people. Even I was a recipient of their prayers when in a near-death situation. For this, I am very grateful. However, I get a hint that a church may be a status quo church when I hear the pastoral prayers. In most cases, this prayer is directed mainly to the church community's concerns. Very important, I admit. Rarely, do we hear prayers for the missionaries and Christians suffering in the global community.

Recently, I was in a church which had an open prayer time in the service. People made their requests to the pastor. "Pray for me that I get another job." "Pray for Charlie to make a smooth transition to his new assisted-living home." "Pray for my aunt Susie that she has a safe trip from Rochester." These were some of the requests. Thank God the pastor included broader and more serious concerns in his pastoral prayer.

I once said hello to a family friend at my church one Sunday. She said, "Please pray for my daughter taking final exams in college and that she has a safe ride home."

I thought to myself, "Pray for Charlie's smooth transition? Pray for a daughter's good college grades?! Don't they know about Florence Hosea, a fifteen-year-old Christian girl from Nigeria who was kidnapped, raped, and forced to wear a Muslim hijab so no one would recognize her? Or David Shestikov who came to Christ after a dramatic conversion and later pastored a small church in Uzbekistan who was arrested and tortured for four years in prison, being separated from his wife and family? Or the hundreds of other Christians who lose their lives, limbs, and property every day serving the Lord in difficult places in foreign countries?" Then we pray for good grades and Charlie's smooth transition! Come on! The priority of the status quo church are so self-absorbed, we are blinded to the real prayer needs of the suffering church.

I was beginning to get caught up in this introspection myself, and I had to pray for forgiveness. Status quo-ism is like putting a frog in warm water and turning up the heat. Before you know it, it overcomes you. Then it's too late. The leadership is failing this congregation. This will be pointed out as I continue in this chapter.

This church is everything I always wanted in a church, except that the church is very static. It is glowing brightly but not going. After being there a year, I noticed that the pews were half empty. Remembering Lou Vanderplate, knowing that there is a very large poor African-American community only four or five miles away and that I had a forty-four-passenger school bus that was not used on Sundays, I approached some elders in the church with my Vanderplate idea. I had my CDL bus driver's license so it would cost the church nothing. I thought we could be conductive to the poor community.

Well, after a meeting with several elders, one elder laughed, and the other said, "It's not our style." After that, some people suggested that I run for elder. But I didn't want to be divisive. I was shown the door from two other evangelical churches for my "crazy" suggestions. I didn't want this church with great people and correct preaching to do the same. I tried my plan one more time at summer vacation Bible school for church children. I had the bus, and it was not used in the summer. What an opportunity to bring city kids to the gospel and a missed opportunity to invite their parents to a closing program where each child would be presented a certificate and their parents would be invited to church on Sunday! I would have been glad to drive the bus and take them home again after coffee hour at my expense, but once more I was shot down.

The reasoning at this time was that there would be "too many people to feed." I said I'd pay for their food all week, but no one would look me in the eye. I knew they were searching for another excuse. They just did not want to do it. I felt very sad. I didn't want to miss this great opportunity. I thought to myself, why can't they see "the fields ... are [black, Hispanic and] white already unto harvest" (John 4:35, ASV). I knew right then that I didn't want to become a member of a blended church. I would support the church with my offerings and my family, and I would volunteer to help in projects, but I was through making "divisive" suggestions.

Sometimes the blended church actually goes against the gospel mission. Case in point: our school had a number of Chinese students that were either Buddhist or atheists. Having a church requirement for them, I invited several to our church that Sunday. It just so happened that our pastor was on or about his tenth week speaking on the Book of Revelation. In the course of his sermon, he depicted Jesus's coming again like a monster coming out of the sea holding a tree where he had one foot in the ocean and one foot on dry land. He went on to describe Jesus with a flaming sword coming out of his mouth and eyes of fire. I was horrified that this was the first introduction for my students of who Jesus Christ was! Now Revelation is a great book, teaching about judgment in the last days but not on Sunday morning with new believers in attendance! I thought this message is fine for mature Christians—it's the meat of the Word. Far more appropriate in evening service or in adult Sunday school.

The gospel was what my students needed. I talked about this to my pastor after the service, and he just smiled but had no answer. This was a clear message to me that nothing would change his preaching schedule. This was a critical setback for me to communicate the love of Christ for these students. When talking with my Chinese agent about this, he said, "This is what they are taught in school; that Christianity is a cult. Now your pastor proved it to them." I could never invite them back to my church again.

Why is this such an important issue with me? Because Jesus said to the church, "I would thou wert cold or hot. So then because thou art lukewarm, and neither cold nor hot, I will spew thee out of my mouth" (Revelation 3:15-16, KJV). In other words, it's better to have both feet in the status quo bucket than to have one foot in the status quo bucket and then to pretend to have one foot in the crucified bucket. Note the reason why Jesus says this is because these people are secure in their status-quo-ism. "I am rich, and increased with goods, and have need of nothing" (Revelation 3:17, KJV) Note the Scripture does not say "wealthy" but "rich." This is exactly what a status quo Christian is: rich in safety, security with his nice home, good job, pension, and not willing to risk it for anything. Get ready to be vomited! This is exactly why blended churches have no mission zeal. "What? Me go? What? Me lose my security?" That's why I call these churches static, status quo, blended churches.

I am not blaming the good people of my church for this mission failure. Without proper shepherding, these leaders keep the flock in the sheep pen, fattening them on correct doctrine, not allowing them to go to green pastures that are "white unto harvest." Dogs don't bark at parked cars, only moving ones. Our church doesn't move out of the sheep pen, I believe because its leaders are afraid of the "dogs" of insecurity and low finances that may bite their ankles. This is sad leadership because the Scripture says, "For unto whomsoever much is given, of him shall be much required: and to whom men have committed much, of him they will ask the more" (Luke 12:48, KJV).

I thought of the words of John Stott—the church exists; by mission as a fire exists by burning. "Sell what you have, give it to the poor, take up your cross, and follow Me." Static or conductive, status quo or crucified, safe or risky? "So [crucified] send I you to labor unrewarded." "Can these [dry] bones live?" (Ezekiel 37:3). Can Laodicea become Smyrna? (Revelation 2:8-11, 3:14-22). Oh God, revive us again.

The monkey is on my back again. I cannot understand why churches with the great Biblical, reformed content, for the most part, have no mission zeal. You would think that with great theology, that brings you closer to the character of Christ and His passion for the lost in the world, would come great missionary fervor. Churches that don't dot their i's and cross their t's strictly in Reformed ways (mostly Arminian) are some of the most passionate for local and foreign missions. Bethel Gospel Assembly, for example. I don't know at my age if I will ever see that monkey lifted off my back.

"Are ye able," said the Master, "To be crucified with Me?"
"Yea," the sturdy dreamers answered, "To the death we follow Thee:"
"Lord, we are able,"—our spirits are Thine;
Re-mold them, make us like Thee, divine.
—Earl Marlatt

Revive us again; Fill each heart with Thy love;
May each soul be rekindled With fire from above.
Hallelujah! Thine the glory. Hallelujah! Amen.
Hallelujah! Thine the glory. Revive us again.
—William P. Mackay

Note: These hymns cannot be sung in our church. If they could be, the situation may have been different.

CHAPTER XVII

MIRACLES ON FLEURY ROAD

Now unto him that is able to do exceeding abundantly above all that we ask or think, according to the power that worketh in us, Unto him be glory in the church by Christ Jesus throughout all ages, world without end. Amen (Ephesians 3:20-21, KJV).

Now I had a dilemma of my own. I wanted to give my kids the opportunity to go to a Christian school, and I needed land to operate a legitimate high school, one that could eventually give kids an equivalent education with the public schools, i.e., sports, music, and a quality campus. I only had one acre and a very small building. I would not do this project without more land. There were 150 acres around me that couldn't be subdivided. The price was $180,000 plus the $50,000 or $60,000 I needed to get the school opened added up to $240,000 at the least. The bank wanted all my directors to sign personally on the mortgage. Two directors, who were financially substantial, quit. The rest of us were just working stiffs and had no real assets. As for me, I had $40,000 in my savings account, left over from cattle and equipment sales. I put all of it into getting the building up. Plus I was in the process of applying for a mortgage on my house to get some funds to complete it. This was about the same situation I was in with the flight school purchase. But I lacked two things. I had no money and little potential income to pay a mortgage even if I could get one. Over half my students in the new school would pay no tuition. Too much risk, I was told by many.

I went to bed that night thinking, "Is pursuing this dream really worth it?" I can remember staring at the ceiling and the words of Ralph Winter rattling around in my head, 'the value of the goal.' I thought, can this little, potential school being built to teach hundreds of young people to serve God with their lives be a reality? I thought, could that school have potential to teach young people a liberal arts education founded on a correct theological foundation that would graduate Christian kids with the tools, education, vision, and courage necessary to explain the gospel to a sinful world? I thought, is this a worthy goal? Answer, yes! Worth any risk? Answer, yes! Yet the problems loomed. I prayed, "Lord, I want to be on the right side of the 'but' here. However, what is the way out of this dilemma?" I continued thinking this was the same predicament I was in with the flight school. Trying to get a loan with no assets or guarantors to offer as collateral. However, in this case, the price was way above market value. I thought, what had helped me back then? I remembered my obstacle course experience. "Be convinced your goal is worthy. Go against the crowd. Risk it all. Attack every obstacle with wisdom and boldness and trust the Lord."

I dozed off for a couple of hours, and the Lord woke me up with a wild idea. Could this crazy plan work? I'll give it my best try. All anyone can say is no. But (on the right side of the 'but') if it's God's plan, I had the faith to believe that there would be no 'no's.'

I rushed to the bank. At eight forty-five a.m. I caught the banker just going into the door. I said, "I've got an idea!" We sat down at his desk.

"What have you got?" he said.

I said, "You want the outstanding balance of the property owner's debt for the land, $180,000?"

"That's what we want," he said. "The present owner owes $110,000 in principle payments, $40,000 in interest payments and $30,000 in penalties. Total, $180,000. What's your idea?"

Well, I said (with my heart in my throat), "If the owner would come up with $25,000 and you would forgive the penalties and interest, we could assume the principle."

He leaned back in his chair and said, "Sonny, we may forgive some penalties, but banks never forgive interest. And why would the owner come up with money anyway? He's going to lose the property. But if you want to pursue this crazy idea, here's the owner's phone number and his name, Nathan Spells."

Well, I got to first base on a very close play! Now, could I steal second? I immediately called Mr. Spells. I explained to him my vision for a Christian school and that I needed the property for athletic fields and future development. I told him I thought we could work a deal out with the Federal Land Bank. He said, "Come on down and see me tomorrow." So early the next morning, I got to his office at a high rise on Fifth Avenue, took the elevator up several floors to his offices. He had beautiful views of the East River and all the activity going on there. I was invited into his very large office. He was an older man, perhaps in his 70s. (I later found out that Nathan was one of the original signers of the Declaration of the Establishment of the State of Israel.) I sat down in front of his very large desk. (I remembered the words of General Patton: "Audacity, audacity, audacity.") I told Mr. Spells that if he would come up with $30,000 to $35,000 that the bank would forgive all penalties and interest and I would take over the principle payments. He studied my proposal mentally for a few moments. Then he got up from his chair, came around to me. I got up also. He gave me a big bear hug and said, "My wife and I are very ill. We do not want to go through a major litigation. I will do your deal." Wow!

I stole second safely.

I drove as fast as I could to the bank. I caught the banker just coming out the door to go home. I told him what Nathan has said. I told the banker that if they forgave the interest and penalties that he would come up with $30,000 to close the deal. The banker said, "I'll talk to you tomorrow."

The next morning he called me. "Let's go down to see Spells. Be at my office at ten thirty." Wow! A chance to get to third base and maybe even home. So with two other bankers, we piled into his little Volkswagen Beetle and headed for New York City. Getting to Nathan's office about noon, they told me to wait in the lobby, and the three bankers went inside to talk to Nathan. I waited for about forty-five minutes. When the door opened, they all came out shaking hands. The bank forgave all penalties and interest and Nathan came up with over $35,000.

I made it to third safely. But I wasn't home yet. The banker said, "We have a deal, but we want you to come up with $10,000 to clinch the deal." Would I get stuck on third?

I rushed back to my home office and called an emergency directors meeting. I explained to them what had happened. I needed $10,000 to get the property and thus the school. I was broke! I had cleaned out my savings account to build the building and only had enough in checking to feed my family for a week. All my other directors said, "No, we can't do it." Wow! Could I be stuck on third? Would the game be over?

With a heavy heart, I had to call the bank the next day. I told him my directors couldn't come up with the money and I had drained all my savings to put in our new building. "New building?" He said, "I'll be out this afternoon to see what you're doing." He came out about three p.m. that day, looked all over our "new" unfinished building. He said, "If you cut out of your property at least one acre and the building and attach it to the

Spells property, I will accept it as the $10,000 down payment." Wow! I had almost got picked off at third! But God hit me home; we won the property. A miracle happened on Fleury Road!

I immediately went to my planning board and got the one acre cut out of our property and gave it to AEF who would be the new owner. In about two weeks, the bank called to tell me the paperwork was ready. I had no John Traphagen now. I would have to sign and guarantee on the new mortgage myself. Now I had to figure out how to pay this monthly payment—about $1,500 and the mortgage I put on my house, $450—totaling about $2,000 a month with no foreseeable income! Providentially, both closings were late in July, so no payments were due until September. I had one month to finish the school's interior and get the C.O. (Certificate of Occupancy) to open on September 6. I had one month to sell two lots on the north end of the property to get funds to pay the mortgage. The race was on!

Once I made the announcement to the community that we would open on September 6, people began to come out of the woodwork to help us get open! Partitions went up. A volunteer electrician wired the place, insulation was put in, sheetrock up and taped. Sal Napolitano made doors. A church school donated wooden desks. Several ladies showed up to paint. We had twenty-seven students registered for September. Fourteen local kids and thirteen Conquest kids form the inner city. Mom and I hired three teachers to teach math, literature, and Spanish. We had one parent volunteer to teach history. Mom would teach science and English, and I taught four levels of Biblical studies. Textbooks began to arrive, a telephone was installed, blackboards went up, and a parent volunteered to be school secretary. We were almost set to open.

With one week to go, I thought I would invite the building inspector in for a preliminary inspection. He did his inspection and said, "Everything looks okay, but there are two things you are missing. A fire alarm system and a furnace."

I argued, "But it's a small building. Yell anywhere, and we are out in ten seconds. Plus, it's August, and we don't need heat."

"I am sorry." He said, "That's the code."

So I immediately called P&N Alarm Systems. I told them my predicament. They said, "Because it was a small building, they could do it over two days." Then I threw in what I thought would be the dampener. I had no money to pay them. (I was already dipping into our family's food money.) P&N said, "You can pay us over time." Wow! They didn't even know who I was! Thank you, God.

Next, I called Ken Schlopak, our local fuel oil and heating company. "Ken, can you find me a used horizontal hot air furnace?" I explained to him my predicament.

He called me back that day and said, "A horizontal unit is hard to find used. I can't find one. I can get a new one for $3,500. Do you want me to order a new one?"

"Ken, I am broke and under this deadline."

He said, "Well, you have one in your house." So Ken gave me two days and his men took my furnace out of my house, cut a 4x8 hole in the school's roof, put it in, hooked up the fuel lines, put 500 gallons of fuel in the tank outside the building, hooked up the electricity, turned it on, and it worked, two days before we were to open. (The ducting was not in yet, but the heat was in!)

The Tuesday after Labor Day, we opened—thirty-four of us. Everybody arrived at eight a.m. The inspection for the C.O. was scheduled to be at ten a.m. so at nine forty-five a.m. we all had to stand outside the building and wait for him to show up. When he came, he was thorough. He set the fire alarm off, made sure we had exit signs on all our doors and rooms. He then turned the thermostat up and listened to see if the furnace would come on. It did! He wrote out the certificate of occupancy and the 1986-87 school year began! As far as I was concerned, the second miracle had occurred. One more was about to happen.

Chapel Field Christian School, 1986

The reason I felt so strongly about having the surrounding property was to have land for athletics and future development. We could not do that on one acre. God had given me a vision for greater things. However, that property, though very beautiful with large fields and woods was not suitable at that point for athletic fields. The one major field, about forty-five acres, rose from the south at about a twenty-degree slope to a high point in the middle and gradually sloped down about 1500 feet to the Dwaarkill River. You couldn't have a soccer field or a baseball field on a twenty-degree slope.

About the time of the closing on the property, a local gentleman, Al Teplitz, called me. He had a small herd of mixed-breed cattle and wanted me to upgrade them. We became good friends because I not only helped him with his cattle, but I secured for him a large bank loan for his next engineering project. It just so happened that Al had an excavating company. He did major excavating like highways and large earth moving projects. So after lunch one day I asked him if he would come out and look at our land to see what it would cost me to get a small playing field area. We rode around the property in my 1948 Jeep and stopped on the hill overlooking the river. I said, "Al, how much would it cost to flatten a place for a soccer field?" He looked. The size of the cut-down needs about twenty feet to level the ground, then he paced off 700 feet needed for a regulation soccer field, did some mental calculations and said the cost would be about $100,000 to $126,000. Wow! That's more than I paid for the property! I gave up on that idea.

About two weeks later, Al called me. "I've got about two weeks between jobs, and I don't want to lay off my crew. I'll give you ten days if you pay my crew, moving the equipment, and fuel. What I get done, I get done."

I said, "Yes!"

Later, I asked Al what he thought that would cost. "$8,000 to $10,000," was his reply. I thought, just like Irwin Lampert, I'd give up ten percent for a miracle. I had faith that God would help me get the money somewhere.

Brian Sebastian, of Team 100, leaning on one of the giant "Yo'uts" tires.

Al moved in his equipment—three D8 Caterpillar bulldozers, two giant earth movers (they call them "yo'uts" or "pans," one bulldozer pulls them, and another pushes it; when full they move the dirt to the other location).

He then stripped off all the topsoil, put it into four giant piles on four corners of the field, cut down the hill, and leveled off a playing field. Bulldozers put the topsoil back over the area, and we had a soccer field. They had to spend over two weeks on the project. I was getting nervous about the money. Al said, "Anything else you want done while I got the equipment here? I've got three more days and I ain't coming back."

"Well," I said, "I could use a baseball field next to the soccer field." So Al and crew went to work again. This time they made an eight-foot cut and moved the dirt 500 feet away to level the field by the river. Al spent almost a month on that job. I was very nervous. When his last equipment rolled out, I asked him "How much do I owe you, Al?"

He said, "I know what you're trying to do here. Give me $3,000." Wow! I felt like giving him a big hug, but Al wasn't that kind of guy. Like me, a thank you and a handshake would do.

Well, I had a piece of land under contract for sale on the other side of the river. I took that deposit right down to Al. Here's what I had for $3,000. A 750'x250' Olympic class soccer field, a 325-foot-down-the-lines baseball field with a 400-foot center field, and both fields ready for seeding. My third miracle in trying to get this school opened. Others would explain it, "Well, the bank was under pressure, so they helped you make a deal. All businesses face challenges trying to stay open. And as far as the fields are concerned, Al was just being practical, trying to keep his people going." Well, my naysayers didn't know the intrigue and odds of bringing the bank and Nathan together on my crazy plan. They didn't know how providentially everything fell into place fifteen minutes before we were due to open. And thirdly, they didn't know about the wear and tear it cost Al to repair his equipment after thirty days of grading it out on our property. These were clearly acts of divine intervention. If God hadn't acted, I would still have my arm up a cow's butt trying to improve what God had already made perfect. I believe we had three miracles on Fleury Road.

> *Great things He hath taught us, great things He hath done,*
> *And great our rejoicing through Jesus the Son;*
> *But purer, and higher, and greater will be*
> *Our wonder, our transport, when Jesus we see.*
>
> *Praise the Lord, praise the Lord, let the earth hear His voice!*
> *Praise the Lord, praise the Lord, let the people rejoice!*
> *Oh, come to the Father, through Jesus the Son,*
> *And give Him the glory, great things He hath done.*
>
> *—Fanny J. Crosby*

CHAPTER XVIII

CHAPEL FIELD

Therefore shall ye lay up these my words in your heart and in your soul; and ye shall bind them for a sign on your hand, and they shall be for frontlets between your eyes. And ye shall teach them your children, talking of them, when thou sittest in thy house, and when thou walkest by the way, and when thou liest down, and when thou risest up (Deuteronomy 11:18-19, ASV).

"The law teaches us we need the gospel of grace; the gospel of grace teaches us we need the law."
—Wm. Spanjer III

A principal of a high school! What was I thinking? I had no educational courses in college, no administration courses, no experience teaching and supervising kids in an academic setting ever! With all the confusion of getting things ready, I had not even read books on the subject of education let alone Christian education. What was I thinking? Now I would really have to lean to fly by the seat of my pants. So I started to teach myself to be a teacher and an administrator. The words of Deuteronomy 11:18 came to my mind: "Teach them to your children," and "my words—teach them."

First, keeping these words in mind, I knew I was dealing with some covenant young people (those raised in Christian homes, thus under the covenant of God's promises to bless believing parents and their children throughout all generations—Acts 2:39; Genesis 17:7; Psalm 22:30, 72:5; Jeremiah 32:39; etc.) and I knew that they would be blessed by the Lord. I was also dealing with young people that were strangers to God's covenant promises, kids that had never really heard the gospel message at all. So I designed a program and schedule that I thought would meet both needs. We would have chapel every morning for thirty minutes where the gospel would be preached in the form of a devotional, challenging students to accept Jesus Christ as Lord and to serve Him with their lives. Next, we gave teachers the mandate to teach all subjects with Jesus Christ as the center and author of that subject; this mandate from Colossians 1:16, where the Scripture says, "For by Him were all things created that are in heaven and earth, visible and invisible, whether thrones or dominions or principalities or powers, all things were created by Him and for Him."

This would be the central point of our academic program. Considering that in government (public) schools, a student from K-12 gets 15,000 hours with God out of the curriculum. That's ninety percent more time than a young person spends in church and about seventy percent more time than he or she spends in activities time with their family, fifteen thousand hours of constant pounding that God has nothing to do with this world of your education. It's called the secular (atheistic) education, far from Biblical education and far from what our Founding Fathers wanted public education to be.

Spanjer host home.
We had many host homes; these are boys that stayed with our family:
(l-r) Shawn Elmore, Team 103—Jersey City, Lateef Meyers, Team
105—Newark, NJ, Bill Sr., Bill Jr. and his girlfriend (and future wife)
Kristina Bivens, Manny Thompson, Team 105—Newark, NJ, Stephen
Spanjer, my wife Kathleen, Tim Spanjer, Kristy Spanjer, Dan Spanjer
and David Julien, Team 100—Harlem

Next, I wanted the Biblical program to be comprehensive in nature. I took all my college courses and rewrote them for high school level. Salvation history (Progress of Redemption) for freshmen, knowing that the theme of the Bible was, 'I will be your God and you my people (Leviticus 26:12). I wanted to show students how people can become God's people. This is the story of personal and national redemption lived out in the lives of the great heroes of faith in the Old Testament (Hebrews 11); Jesus Christ working out the redemption of His people, the study of the Individual (Abraham), the Family (Isaac, Jacob, and Joseph), and the Nation, starting with Moses and going through the Prophets.

The second year (sophomore year), it would be theology, a study of who God is, who man is, who Christ is, and who the Holy Spirit is. This would be a doctrinal study of the great theologies of Reformation truth and the great thinkers that produced the Reformation and promoted it down through the years.

In their junior year, students would take church history, starting where we left off in Progress, studying Christ's incarnation—God with us, His ministry—a demonstration of His divinity, His atonement—the full and free payment of our sins, His resurrection—victory over death for you and me, His proclamation, "Go ye into all the world and preach the gospel," His ascension to power and glory over His kingdom, and finally His prophesied second coming to judge all nations and those who do not accept the gospel. Finally, this course would study the church down through the centuries, the great creeds, the councils, the Reformation, the heroes of Reformation truth, the Christian principles America was founded upon and the faith of the men that fought for our freedom and wrote our Constitution.

In their fourth year, seniors would take up apologetics, making a defense of the Christian faith to our culture, studying the philosophies of our day—secular humanism, existentialism, etc. I threw in a few electives like hermeneutics (to strengthen my students' belief in the Bible, i.e., that it is our sole authority for our faith and how we live) and an ethics course focused around how we should live with others, using R.C. Sproul's great little book *Developing Christian Character*. Ethics is a course nowhere to be found in public school. Sad!

I felt this academic program, if taken seriously by my students, would prepare them well for the challenges they would face in college and would fulfill the mandate I had from the

Lord to "lay up my words in your heart and teach them to your children."

My next concern was in the environment. That was primary. Right away, I formed an honor code. As part of that code, I had zero tolerance for language and bullying. I had a sign on my desk, "Wise guys need not apply" and a policy—two strikes and you're out! This policy took a toll on us financially and on our public relations front. I had to kick out several teachers' kids, several pastors' kids, a prominent donor's kid, and my building inspector's kid right when we were on a major building project. Some parents complained, "As a Christian school, you're not being loving or compassionate." One parent, very irate over her son being asked to leave our school, threw this up at me.

I said to her, "If you want compassion, see your pastor. If you want character, teach your child to obey the rules at Chapel Field. We are in the character-building business. We are a standards-based school, not a church."

Our parents don't pay public school taxes plus private school tuition to have their children in a public school environment where fighting, bullying, language, and drugs are the daily routine. Our parents don't want someone sitting next to their student telling him or her bad things to do. I felt it was my job to keep the environment free and clear of that trash. A family environment. And I knew kids wanted that too. To be successful in life, students need to know boundaries. If some have to follow them and others (because of the parent's standing in our community) don't have to, the standards become irrelevant. You may have the best teachers in the world and the very best curriculum ever offered, but if your students think that some rules don't apply to them, or think they apply to some and not to others, then they will think your teaching is a joke also. A poorly disciplined school is self-defeating.

I had a student transfer to us from another Christian school. She was in eleventh grade. During the family's school tour and visit, I was going over the honor code with her before she registered. I always did this with new students because some would not want to come when they knew the rules. I held that the honor code was to be followed in or out of school. One prospective student told me, "I don't want the school in my private life."

I told that student, "When you accept Christ, you don't have a private life." Another $4,000 gone.

Another girl said to me, however, "I like the rules." Then she asked, "Are they for everyone?"

I said, "They are for my children, my teacher's children, and everyone here."

Then she related a story about her previous Christian school. She said, "A girl in my class this year got pregnant. She was a daughter of one of the elders in the church. Everybody in the school administration kept it a secret, but all the students knew what was going on. It was covered up, and she was allowed to graduate. This same thing happened to my friend who was a senior at the time, and she was kicked out just before graduation. The rules were a joke. That's why I'm here."

God is serious about your behavior. At Chapel Field, I gave kids with attitudes one warning: If it happens again, you are gone. I have had many students in this situation say they are very sorry and some even stand up in chapel and confess to the whole school body what they did and say they were sorry for letting others down. That's all that God asks for, repentance. The proof will be that it doesn't happen again. I had a teacher come to me one day in tears. She said that she swore in class and didn't think she could go back in that classroom again. I said, just go back tomorrow and apologize to the class for your poor choice of words. Kids are very resilient and forgiving, plus you will set a very good example of humility. God knew how many times I have had to apologize to my class over the thirty years I taught for faux pas I've made. Teachers are human and must be repentant too.

A third thing I insisted on was regular church attendance by all staff, students, and faculty. Students had church assignment forms to be filled out during church services, noting hymns sung, the Scripture texts read and the sermon outline. I wanted to make sure kids were paying close attention to the service. These forms were graded and would count as a test grade for their Biblical studies course. I started a Youth Conquest with Christ team on campus and included a Matthew Twenty-five, "To the least of these My brethren" emphasis. This was for students that were serious about their faith and were considering serving God with their lives, being a disciple. This was not a "go-bowling-have-pizza group but kids dedicated to Christ's mission. They met weekly, prayed and planned human needs projects in our community, visiting nursing homes, singing gospel hymns, visiting the V.A. hospital, reading Scripture and praying with patients, even planning overseas missions trips in the future. I wanted to teach Christian kids the discipline and routine of doing outreach with the gospel message. Perhaps when they would get in churches as an adult, they could encourage them not to be status quo congregations. This was my structure and hope for Chapel Field students. So, we were off and running.

It got real cold early winter of '86. By Thanksgiving, with no heat in our house, we were huddled around a potbellied stove in our kitchen, eating and doing homework. These were trying times. I got a call from Ken Schlopak, "I found a furnace, almost brand new. It's now in a new home that the owner just purchased, and he wants to change from hot air heat to board heat."

Knowing I had not money at that time, I asked, "Ken, how

much will it cost?"

Ken said, "I'll give it to you." Wow! I knew Ken could have sold it for about $2,000 or $3,000. So, the next week, Ken and crew put the furnace in, and we had heat! God bless you, Ken!

One day a few girls came to me and asked, "Why is our school called 'Chapel Field?' How did you get that name?" So I decided to do a chapel devotional on how that name came about. For my text that day, I used a very short Scripture verse, "And, behold, the veil of the temple was rent in twain from top to the bottom; and the earth did quake, and the rocks rent (Matthew 27:51, KJV)."

The story goes back to my 1956 deployment to the Mediterranean. The admiral told me to take his car to Portsmouth, and the ship would be there in ten days. So I drove off the main highway into the countryside, working my way down from Scotland to London. I visited farms and stayed in country inns. It was great. I arrived in London on the eighth day (London was about a one-and-a-half-hour drive from Portsmouth), so I took a day to see the sights of London. One site that particularly interested me was Westminster Cathedral. It was massive. The sanctuary, I estimated, had a 100-foot ceiling and was at least 150 feet long. All the stonework amazed me. I noticed as the guide took me around that there were small rooms lining both sides of the sanctuary. I asked my guide what these rooms were. He said they were small chapels where people could come away, pray, and meditate. This thought stayed in my mind for many years.

In the old economy (Old Testament), only the high priest could go behind the giant veil in the sanctuary that separated the Holy of Holies from the outer room called the Holy Place. He would enter the Holy of Holies once a year to make atonement before God (His presence was there) for the sins of the people. Only the high priest was permitted behind the veil.

He even had to tie a rope around his leg so the other priests could pull him out if the presence of God overtook him or killed him. When the final atonement (paying for our sins) took place through Jesus Christ at the cross over 1,000 years later, the veil in the Temple sanctuary rent in two ("And, behold, the veil of the temple was rent in twain from the top to the bottom; and the earth did quake, and the rocks rent"—Matthew 27:51, KJV), signifying that everyone would have access to God because the debt we owed to God by believers was paid in full. The sanctuary now became the whole world! Everyone in the world had access to God (Hebrews 4:16). Years later, when we wanted to set up a Christian school, I thought about Westminster Cathedral and how the little chapels were in the side of the larger sanctuary. I thought our school was like those little chapels, small places within now the greater sanctuary of the world where young people could come, be protected, learn, pray, and prepare to enter the greater sanctuary of God. We had large fields, which represented the "fields white unto harvest," thence, Chapel Field.

In Protestantism, we view Christ as the center of our lives, the hub, so to speak. All activities of life—work, family, church, vacations, and other interests—are spokes from that hub. This in contrast to Catholicism that sees man as the hub, the center. Work, family, church, and other activities spoke out from man. However, at Chapel Field, we demanded that our students take Christ into all of the activities of the day, even sports, music, and art. In music, I had great Christians directing the music programs and keeping Christ dominant. Cynthia Vaughn, Judy Svenson, Elaine Simpson, and later Eric Parks (a nationally known trumpeter with the Jimmy Sturr Orchestra) kept our music program Christ-centered and always glorifying our Savior. In sports, yours truly coached all of them—boys and girls— for about five years. After that time, my boys Bill IV (Bill Jr. we called him for the sake of the press) and Dan took over varsity sports. How humiliating. Coaching varsity sports for a number of years and then being demoted to coaching junior high (modified) sports! But those kids were great and needed a Christ-centered program also.

Side note: We graduated two students in the '86-'87 school year—Pandy Linder and Debra Christine. The next year, Bill Jr. transferred to Chapel Field from Pine Bush High School. He was our only graduate in the second year, 1987-88. Pastor Ezra Williams from Bethel Gospel Assembly came up to speak at his graduation. Our little building was packed. His message of inspiration was just what we needed to plow on. At that time, things were very difficult financially. I prayed, "God, just give us five years at this ministry."

With the complexity of paying teachers, trying to sell off some land, regulations regarding the Health Department, the State Education Department, building inspections, transportation (D.O.T.) rules and inspections and then the Athletic Association rules regarding participation, I was overwhelmed. I thought at that time, "Just give me five years, Lord. That would be a worthy effort." Just at that time, Bill Mulderig, because of legal reasons, had to close down the farms. Public auctions took place at all the farms I had managed. I was out of a job, thus no income. In a way, it was a relief not to have to teach, do sports, run the school, and go to Vermont weekly. Having no pay meant that I would have to start paying Mom for her teaching so that we could have food on the table. However, now I had a bigger problem. With no income, how could I pay our town, school, and land taxes? They amounted to about $10,000 per year. Later, when I started to receive delinquency notices and tax sale dates for our home and property, I realized that you never really own property in our country. You just rent it from the government.

We have graduated hundreds of students, some the Holy Spirit guided to see their lives as resources to serve God. Some I had to ask to leave the school and others have not had our message penetrate their souls (yet). However, every student from 1986 until this day recited our motto every day in chapel. The motto made famous by Martin Luther in his latter book *Table Talk* and made popular in Christian circles by R.C. Sproul, *Coram Deo* (In the face of God)—"Living always, in His Presence, under His authority and for His glory, Coram Deo."

There is no power can conquer you
While God is on your side
Take Him at His promise
Don't run away and hide

It is no secret what God can do
What He's done for others, He'll do for you
With arms wide open, He'll pardon you
It is no secret what God can do

— Stuart Hamblen (made popular by Jim Reeves)

CHAPTER XIX

NO MONEY, NO PROBLEM
GOD THE HOLY SPIRIT GIVES THE INCREASE

Were there is no vision, the people perish: but he that keepeth the law, happy is he (Proverbs 29:18, KJV).

Verily, verily I say unto you, Whatsoever ye shall ask the Father in my name, he will give it you. Hitherto have ye asked nothing in my name: ask, and ye shall receive, that your joy may be full (John 16:23-24, KJV).

I am writing this chapter to demonstrate to the reader that principle that follows: never let lack of money prevent you from starting your vision for Christ's kingdom. Sometimes I like to watch *Shark Tank* when I relax in the evening. Many times I've heard "Mr. Wonderful" (Kevin O'Leary) berate a would-be entrepreneur seeking funding for waiting till his invention was perfect before launching it. "Mr. Wonderful" would say, "If you're waiting for your product to be perfect, two things will happen to you. One, your product will be obsolete. And two, you'll be dead," (never accomplishing it at all). What I am encouraging Kingdom entrepreneurs to do is to be convinced that the gospel law is the joy of your heart, i.e. crucified with Christ in your life; to be dedicated to your vision for God; to be patient, have faith, risk it all, work, and sacrifice; to avoid committee advice at all costs; to proceed with brazen boldness, and watch how God the Holy Spirit will accomplish what your flawed ability and meager resources could not do! My message to you is, don't wait! Status quo-ism will overtake you. Don't delay; make no excuses. Go for it, before it's too late. "Only one life will soon be past, only what's done for Christ will last." In this chapter, I will seek to demonstrate how in my experience, this principle is true. But first I want to lay, as best as I can, a Scriptural foundation for my assumption.

R.C. Sproul and other theologians explain the truth that God the Holy Spirit makes up our shortfall in the success of our vision for Christ by making a distinction between the monergistic and synergistic working of the Holy Spirit. The monergistic (*mono-* being "one," *erg* meaning "working," therefore "one working") is seen in our being predestined before time began to be His child (Ephesians 1:5). He (by Himself, one working) predestined us for adoption to sonship through Jesus Christ and in our regeneration in time (being "born again" or "made alive"). This is also monergistic or "one working"—no cooperation on our part (John 1:13). We "were born, not of blood, nor of the will of the flesh, nor of the will of man, but of God" (KJV). Also, John 15:16, "You have not chosen me, but I have chosen you" (KJV). These are the working of God alone, no cooperation on our part. Our justification (declaration of right standing with God), on the other hand, is synergistic.

God gives us faith (Ephesians 2:8-9). We exercise that faith in belief in the risen Christ. That is what the Reformers referred to as "justification." Synergism comes from the same root from which we get the word symphony, two or more working together in concert. Now, when God gives us faith (Ephesians 2:8-9), we work in concert with the Holy Spirit to exercise that faith in belief in the unseen Christ. That is what the Reformers referred to as our "justification (right standing before God) by faith alone." Two cooperating: the Holy Spirit and me. Now the Holy

Spirit begins in me a new life of cooperation "synergistically" to make me more like Christ.

"Well," you might say, "what has all this to do with my vision?" Everything! Because the Holy Spirit cooperates with us, we "are co-workers in God's service" (I Corinthians 3:9, NIV), "working together with him" (II Corinthians 6:1, KJV). Synergistically, He guarantees the success of our vision for Christ. The Apostle Paul puts it this way, "I have planted, Apollos watered; but God gave the increase" (I Corinthians 3:6, KJV). That increase is over and above what my feeble ability and meager resources could produce! Conclusion: once we forsake status quo-ism, get both feet in the crucified bucket, risk it all, and work in cooperation with the Holy Spirit, our vision for Christ cannot fail! Because God gives us, by divine intervention, what we need to cross the finish line. No money? No problem! Get started.

Now, this doesn't mean that God's increase will come automatically. St. Paul said, "workers together." This demands that we must be wise with our resources and assets, sometimes cunning if need be. After all, it was Jesus who said, "Behold, I send you forth as sheep in the midst of wolves: be ye therefore wise as serpents, and harmless as doves" (Matthew 10:16, KJV).

In the beginning, when I had little or no funds to start a building project, I started several without getting town approval. My theory was it's easier to say you are sorry than to get permission. I will give the reader two examples. When I built my first building (the Conquest building, later a school building), I feared not getting town approval because it would be located right next to the Dwaarkill River. I was told, whether true or not, that a structure could not be built within 100 feet of a riverbed. However, I had only 150 feet between the river and a steep hill. I could not get a building and a road in that limited space. We only had one narrow acre. Also, a septic system would have to be engineered at an estimated cost of $5,000 and a site plan costing an additional $3,000. Money I didn't have. So I built it without approval. But when I tried to open a school there, I needed a certificate of occupancy. The building inspector asked for a building permit. I said I didn't have one. He yelled at me. I said, "I'm sorry." He inspected twice and gave me the certificate. I saved $8,000. He could have made me take the place down and start over but election time was coming up, and that publicity would have not gone over well.

Another situation I had to apply my "Sorry Principle" to was supplying water to my new elementary school. I called a well-driller to get a price. He said it would cost $8,000 to $10,000. However, I had water in my bus garage only 200 feet away. I thought, just dig a 200-foot ditch over, and I got water! No cost. But the Dwaarkill River went between the new school and the bus garage. I was told you can't do that. "You would need D.E.C. (Department of Environmental Control) approval." I found out that their approval would involve an environmental impact study costing thousands of dollars and at least a year to perform. I thought, it's only 200 feet. I'll dig it anyway. So I got my good friend Eric Vellenga with his excavator one morning very early, and we dug through the river. I thought no one would know the difference. But just as we were finishing up, a D.E.C. trooper came squealing in. He was very mad. It seemed that the silt from our digging had turned the water downstream a silky gray. A neighbor complained. I was caught. I said, "I'm sorry." But that didn't cut it. He gave me a summons. I appealed in court, before a judge. I said to the judge, "I am sorry, Judge. The water I needed was only 200 feet away, and I had no money for a well." The judge berated me for not going through the "proper channels" and fined me $250. I got my water and saved what could have been over $25,000. I later learned that the penalty for digging in a controlled stream is $25,000 per foot! I didn't use that "I'm sorry" policy very much after that, but I'm glad that the Lord had my back on that one.

I had twelve major projects I desired to complete in my vision of the Lord—nine that God has accomplished to date; three can be accomplished by others if they continue my vision. However, I am disappointed that God may not let me fulfill my vision for Him. I now know how Moses felt when overlooking the Promised Land. It's my own fault. I should have started earlier in life.

I want to show young Kingdom entrepreneurs how, in my experience, God was faithful to His promises in Matthew 16:23-24: "Ask anything in my name ... and ye shall receive it that your joy may be full." I am a testimony to the fact that there is nothing to life more joyous than seeing God give the increase to your ministry for Him. Solomon was right. "He that keepeth the law, happy is he." I would like to show you God's faithfulness on each completed project by noting the following:

Explanation

Project

Estimated costs to complete

Available funds

God's increase

Current value

Project #1: Purchase of Land
Explained in Chapter 17.

Estimated costs to complete	$180,000
Available funds	$0
God's increase	$70,000
Current value*	$150,000

* At the time of the project

Project #2: Athletic Fields
Explained in Chapter 17.

Estimated cost to complete	$125,000
Available funds	$3,500
God's increase	$121,500
Current value*	$200,000

* Al Teplitz did an additional baseball field above his original quote.

Project #3: Conquest and School Building
Explained in Chapter 17.

Estimated costs to complete	$80,000
Available funds	$40,000
God's increase	$40,000
Current value	$225,000

Project #4: Gym and New Addition
Explanation: In 1996-97, our enrollment was 100 students

and seven teachers. We hardly had room to pass each other in our small original building. In church one Sunday, I met a man, Ed Schrader, a retired builder. I didn't know it at the time, but he was a master carpenter. I told him my predicament. He came over the next day. Then we found the real predicament. The school building was bordered on one side by the Dwaarkill River and on the other side by a steep hill. The only way an addition could be built was out the back and over the outdoor basketball court which had a gravel surface that I had built for the boys' basketball team. We could have gone back on our bigger property to build a new school, but that would be cost-prohibitive. A 1,500-foot road over a swampy area and a well (I had taken the water from my house), with underground electricity dug over 2,000 feet long, would have just cost too much money. So Ed and I designed an extension to our present small building, about 15,000 square feet. It would have a 135-foot hallway, ten feet wide, lined with lockers, five classrooms on the north side, a gym 85x45 with a stage on one end, a kitchen on one end and a music room on the other, and boys and girls locker rooms. Upstairs would be a large library and a computer room over gym area and three offices beyond that. The planning board valued this at over $800,000. But I knew with my volunteer help, I could get it done for under half of that. However, I had no money. But I'd been there before. Ed laid out the building, and I started excavating the foundation with

Addition to original school building going up

my old backhoe. Then I got to work on how I would finance the project. But before that, Mike DeVries, a local concrete guy volunteered to do all the foundation flooring and concrete work. We were on our way!

God had given us 150 acres. I knew I wanted to reserve 100 for future development, so I had fifty acres to sell off. That gave me six lots available for sale (the lay of the land prevented us from selling more) at $50,000 per lot. So with the planning board's approval, I started to sell. The bank wanted one lot to reduce my original mortgage, and a road had to be put in, costing $50,000—about one lot's revenue. With the help of Mike DeVries, Ed Schrader, and Steve Shomo (a pastor/carpenter), the addition was up and closed within three months! Sheetrock, insulation, electric, and heat were next. The total cost was $270,000—$530,000 below the building inspector's estimate and $130,000 below even my estimate! After all the available land was sold, I was still short about $70,000. My building supplier, Washingtonville Lumber, said we could pay the balance over time. And we had a new school!

Estimated costs to complete	$270,000
Available funds*	$135,000
God's increase	$135,000
Current value	$800,000

* 3 lots sold for $45,000 each

Project #5: Two Bridges (one covered bridge and one ninety-foot, with ramps, over the Dwaarkill River)

Explanation: We had to build a covered bridge over the stream to allow our students to come into the school from the parking lot where buses let them off. This bridge was sixty feet long with a bench along one side for students to sit and wait for their transportation home. This bridge had a sign when entering, "Enter to Learn" and another when leaving, "Go Forth to Serve." The other bridge was a ninety-foot bridge, eight feet wide, which included ramps over the Dwaarkill River, connecting the high school to our softball fields and proposed new elementary school.

Covered bridge, student entrance to the new addition

Run-over bridge connecting the two campuses and tournament softball field at Chapel Field Christian Schools

Estimated costs to complete	$8,000
Available funds	$0
God's increase*	$8,000
Current value	$8,000

Note: All funds and labor for the project were donated. Thanks to the people listed in the acknowledgments.

Project #6: Additional Classroom Building

Explanation: We just got our new school and our bridges. That's the way God verifies your commitment and vision. And so it went, one project after the other. We started a middle school, so we needed more classrooms. Mike and Ed went to work again. We got seven additional new classrooms. We dedicated that building as the Hoppe Additional Educational Building after my missionary hero, Bob Hoppe.

Additional classroom building, dedicated as
Hoppe Additional Educational Building

Estimated costs to complete	$175,000
Available funds	$85,000
God's increase*	$90,000
Current value	$268,000

* Amount due to donations, volunteer labor by Ed Schrader, Mike and Hank DeVries and my crew.

Project #7: Bus Garage, Equipment Storage Building and Maintenance Shop

Explanation: We had eight finish-cut mowers, six tractors and a baseball/softball field groomer we needed to get under cover, plus a place to store three school buses and a shop for maintenance and repair. So Ed and I designed a 75x48 pole building with six bays thirteen feet high. Included was a pit in the shop area for bus repair.

Bus and maintenance garage

Estimated costs to complete	$125,000
Available funds	$68,000
God's increase	$57,000
Current value	$350,000

Before I started project 8, Ed Schrader retired for the second time. We held an Ed Schrader Night at Chapel Field. All my staff and volunteers showed up. We dedicated the whole facility to Ed, installing a large sign on the front of our building, "The Edwin Schrader Educational Facility." Ed was a giant among men. His personality was reserved, calm, confident, and very humble. He built our school almost single-handedly. He was a genius with figures and the kind of man I would have liked to have been.

Project #8: Elementary School

Explanation: Jesus said, "Prevent not the little children from coming unto me." I wondered how Christian parents could put their little children in a godless school that teaches their child to be godless? After all, a child spends over 6,000 hours from Pre-K to fifth grade in godless schools, being taught that there is no God! What kind of insanity is that? I designed a building with two wings, each 60x48, able to house six classrooms, a kitchen, two bathrooms, and a utility room. These attached to a center building, 54x88, which would house a gymnasium in the rear portion and two classrooms, an office, a library, and a foyer.

Elementary School

Estimated costs to complete	$210,000
Available funds*	$170,000
God's increase**	$40,000
Current value	$875,840

I took out a mortgage for $100,000 to help pay for materials.

** *Amount reflects the work and sacrifice of volunteers described below.*

The town of Shawangunk estimated this building completion at $2,800,000. I built it for a little over $200,000. I had squirreled away about $70,000, I took a bank loan for $100,000 and paid the balance to the lumberyard over one year. The savings were due to Eric Vellenga and his son who did all the excavating at no charge, Mike and (particularly) Buddy DeVries who poured the foundation and floor at no charge, Mike Bonagura who provided the construction crew, Eric McCaffrey who did all the plumbing and heating at no charge. I might add that this building and all of our buildings were built on the backs of my teachers who worked for a pittance compared to public school teachers. Now that's how to build a ministry! His servants sacrifice time, labor, and resources and God makes up whatever shortfall is needed by divine intervention. I am His witness.

I located the school across the Dwaarkill River where it would have its own space, athletic fields, and playgrounds. Now we would have a beautiful campus and a K-12 Christian school. Our little school began to grow. In 2007, our enrollment grew to seventy students in elementary, forty in middle school, and 142 in high school for a total student enrollment of 252. That leads me to my last project.

Project #9: Student Residence (Dormitory)

Explanation: In 2008, clouds were looming on the school's horizon once again. But God was not done with His divine intervention on our behalf once again. The poor economy created by President Obama cost us, over his term as president, 137 students in our high school and middle school programs. This was well over $600,000 a year loss of income. We were having a great difficulty paying our teachers and maintaining our programs at the beginning of that time. I had worked out an austerity plan that would take us back with staff and programs to what we did in the early 90s. This would eliminate about seventy percent of our staff. I prayed, "Oh God, please don't let that happen. We have a dedicated and sacrificing faculty and staff and Mom and I would be devastated to lose them. But if You guide us through this drought, that's the only way I will do it."

That year, 2010, we did notice that the international student registrations began to pick up. Not only was this an answer to prayer but in God's providence, we had two major blessings. First, these students paid over five times what our domestic students paid (and we got it all up front). That eliminated my austerity plans. And secondly, these Chinese students were Buddhists and atheists. Now for the first time, they were hearing the gospel, going to church regularly, and taking Bible courses. Of course, there were problems. They were very rich kids and had some behavioral problems but as soon as they saw we were very serious about faith and behavior, most settled right in and became cooperative. We had many conversions and some baptisms among older students.

God wasn't done providing divine guidance. In 2012-13, our international enrollment grew to about twenty or twenty-five. Where was I going to house these students? On top of that, my Vice President of International Students (Asia) said the following year, we would have thirty-five to forty Chinese students (which was the maximum I would consider for domestic to foreign ratio)! So I grabbed my good friend Chuck Fowler, who was a realtor and we began looking for a large house or a retirement home that would be able to house a number of students. We looked at many, but most needed a lot of work. Then his son, Justin, browsing the internet one evening, found a convent for sale just ten minutes away from our school! The dormitory, including the attached three-story Victorian house, had over thirty rooms and a modern cottage for staff. It was ideal for our needs. However, the asking price was $1,200,000. I learned that there were several offers, much lower than the asking price). So I decided to throw my hat in the ring at $600,000. I didn't have much hope, but I had the Lord. To my amazement, the Little Sisters accepted my offer! I found out later that although some had offered more, the Little Sisters wanted to keep it in Christian hands. Now, where would I get $600,000, let alone a down payment, when I didn't have either? Well, my banker said based on my international student contracts and my appraisal, the

Chapel Field Residence Hall, dormitory attached rear of Victorian

bank would loan me the $600,000 for no money down! We got seven acres at the highest point in the Village of Walden, a gorgeous facility, room for over sixty students with a commercial kitchen, two apartments for staff, a chapel, five additional classrooms, a game room, and a lounge room, plus a cottage with a two-car garage. All for $600,000!

Estimated costs to complete	$600,000
Available funds (mortgage)	$0
God's increase*	$0
Current value**	$700,000

God had given us the funds upon which the mortgage was based.

** *Based on current appraisal.*

These projects spanned over twenty-five years of God's faithfulness to His promises of Matthew 16:23-24. Many other things God answered prayer for us but on our projects, let's sum it up. Total of all projects:

Estimated cost to complete	$1,773,000
Available funds	$440,300
God's increase	$561,500
Current value	$3,576,840

Estimated cost to complete: Mine and my carpenters' estimated cost of materials to complete projects.

Available funds: Funds I squirreled away over the twenty-five years, even these funds were given by God's grace.

God's increase: This amount is mainly from donations, volunteer professional help, other volunteers, suppliers' discounts and the miracles of God, providentially worked out in His timing and in the hearts of the men we were dealing with.

Current value: This amount reflects the current market value at the time of construction or purchase. This figure is a conservative valuation derived from town building based on square foot costs.

Three million, five hundred seventy-six thousand, eight hundred forty dollars ($3,576,840). Quite a return considering our ministry started $110,000 in debt! This is what can happen if you are co-workers together with Christ.

This doesn't reflect how God had taken care of my family. Five times, my house and property have been listed in the newspapers for tax sale. One time I had two days before the auction. I could have lost everything and been out on the street, but God helped me scrape together the $10,000 needed in the nick of time. Times were tough, often down to the last dollar. However, as God was faithful in supplying the needs of our ministry, He was also faithful to my family. God did all this for a country boy like me. No money? No problem!

> *Great is Thy faithfulness, great is Thy faithfulness.*
> *Morning by morning, new mercies I see.*
> *All I have needed, Thy hands have provided.*
> *Great is Thy faithfulness, Lord unto me.*
>
> *—Thomas O. Chisholm*

CHAPTER XX

BEYOND THE CLASSROOM

If ye love me, ye will keep my commandments
(John 14:15, ASV).

*Go ye therefore, and make disciples of all the
nations, baptizing them into the name of the Father
and of the Son and of the Holy Spirit: teaching them
to observe all things whatsoever I commanded you*
(Matthew 28:19-20, ASV).

*Verily I say unto you, inasmuch as ye did it unto
one of these my brethren, even these least, ye did it
unto me* (Matthew 25:40, ASV).

When I've said, "beyond the classroom" I once had a person respond, "Oh, you're writing about sports at Chapel Field." No, I had something bigger in mind. However, I might mention our extracurricular program before going into our mission efforts.

When we started Chapel Field, I joined a Christian school athletic league. It was a disaster: poor excuses for gyms, pastors officiating, surprisingly bad language by opposing players and actual bitter competition. When I say "bitter," I mean bad sportsmanship, teams behaving in an unfriendly manner, not shaking hands after games, etc. It was not for me. After joining the public school league, what a difference—big gyms, professional officiating, bad language was prohibited. Competition was fierce but always friendly with handshakes after games.

We struggled to win games at first but soon became competitive. Our teams have won twenty-five league championships, twenty-four sectional titles, thirteen regional titles and seven New York State championships (six in softball with great pitchers like Julie Schaper and Alyssa Brognano, under the coaching of Bill Jr. and one in baseball with the great pitching of Joey Schlegel under the coaching of Joe Canazon). I felt a little embarrassed by this because I didn't want to be noted for my sports teams but rather for being a true Christian school.

But "beyond the classroom" really refers to my interest in having young people gaining experience and a passion for gospel outreach and those suffering in our local and global community. Our Youth Conquest team at Chapel Field did numbers of local human needs projects, visiting veterans at our local V.A. hospital—reading Scripture to them, singing to them, praying with them and simply befriending them—cleaning streets in our local inner-city community, helping the elderly, and working with Samaritan's Purse Ministry. But I still wanted my students to experience the needs of other cultures, particularly in the Third World.

My secretary at the time was Amy Kumicinski. She had found out about a little orphanage in Nairobi, Kenya, near the Ngomongo slums that had little to no support. I thought this might be a good project for our school to take on. So I called my son, Stephen, who is a missionary in Germany. I asked Stephen to go down to Nairobi and see what was really going on at the orphanage. I wanted to make sure that their director was not driving around in a Cadillac or something. I wanted to make sure that they really needed our help. So Steve went down, lived with the kids for a week, ate what they ate, slept where they slept, pooped where they did, and called me back. "Coach, these are kids off the streets. Some have been eating out of Nairobi's dumps and others have been begging for food. They are squatting on property they don't own, and there are about seventy boys in the orphanage. The director, Philip, lives with them and seems to be a genuine guy. They have a large garden but the problem is there has been a major drought, and they can't grow anything." Immediately I wired a few hundred dollars to Philip and decided to get all of Chapel Field involved in filling a shipping container for Philip and the boys.

Well, I didn't know what I was getting involved in or how to start. This would turn out to be the most complicated and expensive project I would ever undertake. I had a student whose father was Vice President for Norwegian Cruise Lines, so I gave him a call. His name was Joe Assante. "Joe, I have seventy boys with nothing to eat in an orphanage in Njathaini, Kenya, and there is an area-wide drought at this time. I want to send a shipping container with food and supplies to them. Can you help me?"

Joe said, "Sure, I'll give my friend Mark Fromm a call. He's an international shipping agent. We'll see what he can do." The next day, Mark called me and said he was interested in my project. The next thing I knew, Mark made an arrangement with P&O Nedlloyd Shipping Lines for a shipping container under a humanitarian policy by P&O for a fifty percent discount on transportation. He turned me over to Sarcona Transport, and the container arrived at Chapel Field on November 15, 2004. We had three weeks to fill it. The race was on.

I called my friend Brian at Sysco Food Distributors and told him about my seventy starving boys in Kenya. He told me that the company would double whatever we ordered for the container. I ordered $1,000 worth of food supplies and got $1,000 free!

Sysco food deliveries for African container

We were off to a great start. Parents and students came through, over 150 of them, and got behind the project, some gave money; others gave items. We collected hundreds of various items:

- household items, including hygiene supplies and cooking items

- tools and equipment including an irrigation pump and 100 feet of hose (the orphanage had a large pond next to it), a rototiller, chainsaw, carpentry, and mechanical tools and much more

- educational supplies, textbooks, encyclopedias, computers, office supplies

- clothing items, including twenty boxes of mixed donated clothes and over 100 pairs of sneakers (many of which came from unclaimed lost and found items at our school)

- 100 Christmas gifts donated by Chapel Field students

The container was almost full, only about two or three feet on the top of items was still open space. I talked with Philip, and he told me that most boys had to walk six to seven miles to school one way each day. So I put a call out to all the school parents asking if they had a bike they would consider donating to the kids in Kenya that were in dire need of it. The next morning, forty bicycles were dropped off at the school.

40 bicycles showed up

We stuffed them in the space left at the top of the container. The students made a big sign and placed it inside the doors of the container. It said, "Soli Deo Gloria." We closed the door and locked it and called Sarcona to come and pick it up. The whole school and middle school came out to pray with the driver over the container when it was picked up.

All school prayer to send off container

The container left Port Newark on about November 29 and reached Caghliari, Italy about December 25. It left Caghliari on December 29, going through the Suez Canal and arrived in Jeddah, Saudi Arabia to await transfer to the M.S.C. Sudan for expected delivery in Mombasa, Kenya on January 28, 2005. I was worried about three things. Would the container get lost between the two transfers? Would the ship get hijacked by Somalian pirates? And thirdly, since everything operates on payola in Kenya, could the container get from Mombasa to the orphanage intact and without paying enormous bribes to government officials? (Here I had to rely on Pop Suplee's principle) But we had the Lord on our side in this project. I called my son Stephen in Germany again and asked him and his friend and ministry partner Rob Piscatelli (a '94 Chapel Field graduate) to go down to Mombasa and help protect the container and ensure that it gets to the orphanage safely. He made it just in the nick of time, as it was quarantined because of inadequate paperwork. It seems I had not sent an inventory with the shipping manifest for the container. The dock master wanted to unload the container at the dock and count everything in it. I panicked because I knew that once it was opened, we would lose most of the valuable items. Now I had to pull out my old policy of "It's easier to say you are sorry than ask for permission." I said to Stephen, "Just say you are sorry and find out what bribe you must pay to get the container on its way to the orphanage."

Well, Stephen got back to me and said, "Coach, it will take $1,000."

I said, "Pay it."

Container arrives at the orphanage undisturbed

As a side note, two years later, we sent another container to the orphanage. This time I had about $25,000 worth of goods in it and all the paperwork in order. However, the dock master made us unload the container at the dock. He made two piles and said, "This one is for you, and the other is for me." We lost over fifty percent of our goods, over $12,000 worth! That was the last of our container adventures. Everybody is on the take in Kenya. After that, we decided to send money for them to buy items and food in Kenya. They would lack the equipment we could send, but it was far less risky.

While Stephen and Rob were over in Kenya sorting out our first container, I asked them to interview the boys at the orphanage and pick out three. I would offer to those boys a full academic-plus-room-and-board scholarship to attend Chapel Field. They picked three, Gilbert Ndenga, Fanuel Otiato, and Joseph Maina. It took several months of interviews and arguing with officials, but passports and visas were finally issued. They arrived having not ever eaten in a restaurant or even a McDonald's burger.

Three boys from Kenya arrive at Chapel Field, greeted by Coach
(l-r): Fanuel Otiato, Joseph Maina, and Gilbert Ndenga

Well, three years later, the director of the orphanage died under suspicious circumstances following allegations of abuse of the children there. The children scattered. We tried to pick up the pieces by opening our own home in an abandoned house that the government agreed to let us use temporarily. Plus, we opened a school, Chapel Field East Africa, for children of the nearby Ngomongo slums. At that time, these children could not go to school as parents had to pay for education in Kenya. It was a great ministry, feeding and educating ghetto children but it ended in 2014 when the government granted free education to all children in grades K-8. We have continued our orphanage to this date in our government-approved home. However, I don't know how long we can keep it up with no one there to hold the Kenyans accountable. The culture is so different than ours. You send money for certain items, and they spend it any way they want to.

Chapel Field School in Ngomongo ghetto, East Africa

One of the most rewarding things we had done at Chapel Field is our Matthew Twenty-five Relief Ministry. Along with the containers, we have send out many missions teams to foreign countries like Mexico, Honduras, and Kenya. Hearing the life-changing testimonies of these students that have come back after living with impoverished Third World people, hearing how they worked with these people, shared their food, communicated the gospel to them and helped with projects was a great reward for our faculty and staff. It changed these students' lives. Permanently.

(top row, l-r) A child living on streets being begged to come to the orphanage, some boys in the orphanage (note: none have shoes until container arrives), a child searching for food among street garbage
(middle row, l-r) The prized main meal, when they can get it—restaurant leftovers, child at orphanage receiving package, boys anticipating container door opening
(bottom row, l-r) Sysco food waiting for loading onto the container, forty boys on forty bikes

Even more, we now have graduates serving Christ full-time in Alaska, Germany, Spain, Honduras and in many other parts of the world, including many who are serving in ministries in the U.S. This is the icing on the cake for me in this ministry.

We have had almost 700 graduates go through our program. They all know well, and I think miss saying, our motto at Chapel Field, "*Coram Deo*: Living always in His presence, under His authority, and for His glory."

On November 6, 2016, I had a severe stroke, a major aortic stenosis in my heart, an aneurysm in my abdominal artery, and bleeding at the end of my large intestines. I had several surgeries and spent five months in Columbia Presbyterian Medical Center in New York City with my daughter always at my side, sleeping in chairs every night. I left the hospital March 19, 2017, partially paralyzed on my left side, unable to walk without help (and when I do, it's very painful), with kidney disease and not able to eat through my mouth. I am a mess. I'd be in a nursing home playing bingo now if it had not been for my daughter, Kristy, taking care of me day and night. My son Bill Jr. has taken over the day-to-day operations of the schools and is doing a great job. I still keep my hand in the financial area and work on some major expansion projects.

A final note to end this book: Last night I returned from watching our school's spring concert. It was a wonderful event. We held it at Goodwill Presbyterian Church as our small gym could not accommodate our large number of students and their families. When one hundred elementary students (K-6) sang "Jesus Loves the Little Children," I was so moved and thought of the words of Jesus, Prevent not the little children from coming unto Me, for such is the Kingdom of God. And when one hundred and fifty high school kids (grades 7-12) and the concert band ended the program with "Just a Closer Walk with Thee," I thought of the Apostle Peter's words from John 6:66-68, "From that time many of his disciples went back and walked no more with him... Then Simon Peter answered him, Lord, to whom shall we go? Thou has the words of eternal life" (KJV). These children wanted a "closer walk with Jesus." Seeing these 250 young people singing praises to our Lord drew my mind back to the miracles on Fleury Road, where we started $110,000 in debt, with twenty-seven students and five teachers in the 100'x50' building. Now we've grown to over 250 students with over thirty teachers and staff. Small peanuts to some in comparison to major Christian ministries but to those of us laboring on this beautiful 100-acre campus, yet a postage stamp-sized ministry in God's global mega-vineyard, it's a miracle upon miracle. My father's words were true when he said to me, "Bill, do the extra (go beyond your requirements), don't run with the crowd (don't take advice from boards or "groupthinkers"), and don't always play it safe (go for it at any cost)." And over the years, I added one more imperative: Trust in the Lord Jesus Christ with all your heart. The obstacle course proved that advice true. God has certainly "given the increase." I hope this tiny vineyard here has managed His resources adequately. Time will tell when I stand before the Great Judge of the universe and try to give an account of my behavior.

Bill Spanjer III
Solo Christo Gloria

I'll love Thee in life, I will love Thee in death,
And praise Thee as long as Thou lendest me
breath;
And say when the death dew lies cold on my brow,
If ever I loved Thee, my Jesus, 'tis now.

—William R. Featherston

EPILOGUE

OBSERVATIONS

I suppose there are many things I have seen in my eighty-plus years that have upset me, both politically and religiously, but I will mention three here that I feel are most important. One has to do with a grave situation for our country and Christianity and the two others I see as a serious injustice within Christianity. They are **political and religious secular progressivism, groupthink** within the church and **the false narrative of what the "para-church" is**.

Political secular progressivism (P.S.P.). Just as religious secularism sought to drive us into the post-Biblical era, P.S.P. is seeking to drive us into the post-Constitutional era and it has already got a good start. There may not be any turning back now. A democracy is only good as long as its majority are both moral and just. However, in America (as in most of the world) its citizens have given up on, and even viciously, oppose any religious moralism.

Political secular progressivism in America and religious secular progressivism (R.S.P.) are satanic attempts to eliminate both institutions.

By secular progressivism, I mean, to advance change without God. In order to accomplish the change both P.S.P. and R.S.P. must attack the source or founding documents of both institutions. They must discredit these documents to make them irrelevant. In the case of the United States, these founding documents are the Constitution and the Bill of Rights. In the case of Christianity, it is the Holy Scriptures. In 337 B.C., Philip of Macedon coined the phrase, "Divide and conquer." Generals down through the centuries have used that strategy to win victories against their enemies all over the globe. Satan used this strategy very effectively in the mid to late 1800s to divide Christianity in Europe into two factions: modernists (the enlightened of the age of science), and the conservatives (those theologians still believing that the Holy Scriptures are inerrant and divinely inspired). The modernists did this by claiming that the Holy Scriptures are irrelevant because in part, they're just legend. This strategy proved to be a great success. Over 100 years, all of Europe and Scandinavia have become spiritually dead. A few brave souls, like my son Stephen and Jon Romaine, both Chapel Field graduates, and others are trying to reclaim Europe for Christ. Modernism came to America and claimed immediate success in the mainline churches. But as soon as it went out from the Ivy League schools, it received a counterattack and stopped dead in its tracks by the Bible-believing fundamentalists. Protestantism may be divided with all its denominations, but evangelicals are not divided on the issue of Biblical inspiration and the inerrancy of the Scriptures.

One of the important consequences of Luther and the Reformation was the development of Protestant denominationalism. This guaranteed that the church would never again become a centralized "deep church swamp" anymore.

The problem today is that trickledown Christianity, though it revolutionized the Western world for over 2,000 years with its intrinsic benefits of freedom and civilized progress, is no longer effective for an increasing number of Americans. Why is this? Because many churches stopped preaching the gospel, thus destroying the conscience of the people.

Where the gospel is proclaimed, people are converted. Converted people are free and live with inspiration, creativity, righteousness and compassion. This trickles down to society as a whole and all benefit. Though all people may not be true Christians, the gospel through true Christians effects all.

You might ask why I am making such a big fuss about this. It's all history and we know that. Well, Satan is using the same philosophy to "divide and conquer" the United States. When I was a boy and even a young man, we had Republicans and Democrats, liberals and conservatives but we were united in the protection of our Constitution because it was given to us by God, to men who are "endowed by their Creator"—as set forth in the Declaration of Independence. However, political secular progressives say that this document is not relevant to this age. They attack the basic tenants—freedom of speech, right to assembly, the Second Amendment, and our guarantee of religious freedom. No longer is the free exchange of ideas welcome in our heavily tax-supported universities. They used to be bastions of free speech.

The deeper problem is that although political secular progressives don't have the power, at this time, to change the Constitution, they have a new strategy—just ignore it! President Obama made this clear when he said, "I have a phone and a pen." When in power, P.S.P.s will have that loophole to get around the Constitution before they possess the power to destroy it just like religious secular progressives did in the late 1800s to divide Christianity from its founding documents, the Holy Scriptures.

So what must we do to protect ourselves from this anti-Christ movement? Take a page from the evangelicals' playbook when liberals tried to destroy their founding document. Fight it with the gospel. The conscience of our newly formed republic was founded by many devout Christians including John Adams and George Washington, and later advanced by men such as Andrew

Jackson, Abraham Lincoln, and Noah Webster, just to mention a few. These men got their convictions and vision from Christianity. The new republic was inspired by men like George Whitfield, the Wesleys, Jonathan Edwards, the Puritans and from the great preaching of Charles Spurgeon. What did they say that inspired and proclaimed such great Constitution and republic? The gospel, the gospel, the gospel; that God sent His Son into the world to sacrifice His life as a payment for the sins of His people. This by grace alone and appropriated by faith and repentance in Jesus Christ alone. The result: a new people, living in righteousness and love. This is the answer to secular progressivism.

Only that can change the hearts of man to live free and in harmony with their fellow countrymen. This is the antidote for the addiction to secular progressivism. If we don't shout the gospel from the housetops, inject it into our public education institutions, into our liberal church denominations and elect politicians who trust in it, we in America and all humanity are doomed to conflict, hatred and anarchy. A Genesis 6 crisis will loom all over again. I know that all of our Founding Fathers were not devoted Christians (most were Deist) and did not want our nation to be in anyway a theocracy or connected with any religious institution. However, they were all heavily influenced by the gospel and Christianity as spread by those previously mentioned. This particularly the Biblical view of the nature of man, assuring that a despot would never rise from our nation. Our government must be separated from Christianity but Christianity must never be separated from our leaders. This is the answer to secular progressivism.

Our Lord, in the prayer He taught us, says, "Thy kingdom come ... on Earth as it is in Heaven." What is that kingdom that we pray for like? Well, it will be holy, righteous, just, good, merciful and loving, just like the character of God. Pray and proclaim the gospel, now while we have time.

Groupthink. I don't believe that there is anything that prohibits the gospel from going forth in its fullness more than groupthink. Status quo, bureaucrat committees, and elders are placed in positions to oversee and approve local church congregations, their policies and budgets. How can status quo leaders give advice to crucified men and women? It would be like me, a stick-and-rudder guy, on a board, telling John Glenn how to fly a space capsule. It's nonsense. Status quo church "church-au-crats" don't know anything about the commission to the crucified church. There the Apostle Paul gives his pupil Titus the qualifications of elders. "[These elders should be] men who are of unquestionable integrity and irreproachable ("blameless," KJV)" (Titus 1:6, AMP). Unquestionable and irreproachable? How does that match up with status quo men who have their ultimate trust in financial security, safe, and devoid of any risk? If I were a pastor, any candidate for eldership would have to show me two year's personal profit and loss statements (P&L) and a balance sheet with his net worth on it. I would want to know he has both feet in the right bucket before he can give direction to my church and to other Christians.

I was through with committees many years ago. I turn to the Scriptures as my example. "What are you doing, Noah?" says the committee. "Don't you know it hasn't rained ever?" And I am sure the "elders" came to Abram and said, "You don't know where you're going? What are you thinking?" And how about Moses? "We elders don't recommend that you get feisty with Pharaoh. What's the matter with you?" And take Elijah, for example. "The committee recommends that you don't aggravate Ahab. You know, his wife Jezebel might kill you." And then there's David. "The elders got together and feel it's not wise for you to go against the giant Goliath." And what about Rahab?

"The family does not want you to hang that scarlet ribbon from your window. Do you want us to get hung for being a traitor?" And so it goes with Isaiah. And how about Daniel? "The elders recommend that you just get along with Nebuchadnezzar. Eat his food. What's the big deal?" And Esther. "The elders say you'd better not go against Haman or you'll be hanging on his gallows." And there was the leper in a crowd, going face to face with Jesus. The leper colony committee says don't do it. "You have to shout 'Unclean! Unclean!' and stay away for 200 feet. You will be killed." And Martin Luther. "The elders got together and recommend you not hang those 95 Theses on the church door. You know what happened to Wycliffe? He got strangled. And Hus. He got burned at the stake."

And so it goes, down through Biblical and church history. God chooses crucified individuals, men and women, to carry out His redemptive purposes in history. The Scriptures prove it so. Status quo committees and elder boards only inhibit the gospel going forth. My personal experience proved that to be true.

Finally, on this issue, Jesus reminds us in Matthew 6:24 that "No one can serve two masters; for either he will hate the one and love the other, or he will stand by and be devoted to the one and despise and be against the other. You cannot serve God and mammon (deceitful riches, money, possessions, or whatever is trusted in) (AMP)." Money, possessions or whatever is trusted in identifies clearly a status quo Christian. If we are not careful, these will be the people that serve on committees and elder boards—groupthinkers. God never works through these kinds of boards. History has shown that God chooses crucified individuals to carry out His purposes. I don't want to deal with "Ananias and Sapphira." And it is evident that God didn't either. "Show me the meat"—your balance sheet. Convince me both feet are in the right bucket. Then we serve God together.

And a final observation, for this book anyway, **the false narrative regarding the parachurch**. I first heard the definition of a parachurch while in college when one of my professors defined it as "the church that comes alongside the institutional church to help it in its ministry." I thought little about the issue until I was seeking support for my Christian school in 1986. After visiting a number of pastors without success, I asked one pastor why he saw no value in what we wanted to do. He said, "I see value in your program. However, our church does not support parachurch ministries." Another pastor told me, "If you're not under the board of a local church, you're considered a parachurch, and we cannot give you funds." I thought for the first time, what is the church anyway? Now, I am not an ecclesiastical scholar. I am just a jarhead country boy trying to make sense of what I observe in our Christian culture and in relation to the Word of God. But what I observe is crucified people, members of the church of the Lord Jesus Christ begging local bureaucratic status quo "wheat and tare" Christians to help them carry out the demands of the gospel. I thought, actually, the local church is the parachurch coming alongside (when they feel like it) the crucified church of Jesus Christ to help them! Denominations that receive church funds to send out or assist crucified missionaries are paradenominations. The pastors I talked to and my professor got it backward. The local church is the blended parachurch and crucified mission workers are welcomed members of the church of the Lord Jesus Christ.

Let me put it this way. There are normally two classes of people in most local churches. There are first-class members who submit themselves to be under the authority of, in many cases, status quo elders and there are attenders that are "second-class" Christians. These Christians do not want to submit to what may be status quo elders because they don't know really who they are.

Are they really crucified by Biblical standards, unquestionable, irreproachable by Jesus Christ's standards of Matthew 16:24, 19:21, etc. (see Chapter 13 of this book)? Are they true disciples? Have they sold everything, given it to the poor and taken up their cross and followed Christ? Have they risked it all and trusted Christ for their total security? If not, they are status quo and blended at best. The books are not opened for prospective members. I had one pastor, when discussing this subject, say, "You're just prideful for not submitting to those types of elders."

I said, "No. Many years ago, the Holy Spirit caused me to surrender that power to Jesus Christ alone, and I am not willing to surrender it to a human being."

Then the pastor said, "In Hebrews 13:17, it says to submit yourselves to your elders."

I said, "The Bible says in the previous verses that the elders must be crucified and be examples to the flock." Status quo elders are not crucified and not examples to follow or give your authority to.

Second-class Christians, although having been baptized, repentant, made a public confession of their faith and serving God with their lives are members of the church of Jesus Christ, no matter what the local pastor says. But second-class Christians in the bureaucratic church are not allowed to vote or hold leadership positions. And what is the reason for this double standard anyway? William Hendricksen in his great little book *The Covenant of Grace* states, "Never say you are going to 'join the church.' You cannot do this for as covenant members, you are already members of the church" (p. 57).

Jesus and the Apostle Paul come to the same conclusion. "For whosoever shall do the will of my Father who is in heaven, he is my brother, and sister and mother" (Matthew 12:50, ASV). No division here—"For as the body is one" (I Corinthians 12:12,

ASV). "But now they are many members, but one body" (I Corinthians 12:20, ASV). Also see Ephesians 5:30 and Romans 12:4.

A case in point to illustrate this disparity: I know of a church that had a wonderful organ. It was right up front in the church where everyone enjoyed seeing it played every Sunday. Some music people in that church, though well-intentioned, wanted a new organ but it cost (I am told) about $100,000! Well, the elders, and I assume other members in the church, pushed it through. Attenders had no say. This in spite of the hundreds of missionaries fearing for their lives, working in Muslim countries or the thousands of Christian refugees displaced from their homes wondering where their next meal is coming from. Now I do not know whether the funds for the second organ were donated or specifically given for that purpose, but the results were the same. The older, perfectly good organ stands as a monument to the status quo in the front of the church, while the new $100,000 organ sits in the back of the sanctuary where neither the organist nor the organ can be seen. R.C. Sproul might say, "To what purpose is this waste?" A reply from Jesus's disciples after a woman poured a very expensive box of alabaster on his head. "For this ointment might have been sold for much, and given to the poor" (Matthew 26:9, ASV). That's the same argument I am making for the very expensive organ. Jesus also said, "Why troubleth this woman? For she hath wrought a good work upon me." Now if Jesus were here, we should heap all our riches upon Him for He is the King of kings, Lord of the universe. But He is not here now, and the poor are. In the interim, I believe Jesus requires us to use our resources wisely to accomplish His mission He has set before us.

I know pastors, theologians, and congregations are very offended by my closing observations. They will either dismiss me or make complicated Biblical arguments to refute my thoughts. Just show me the text. I've asked many pastors to show me the Biblical text or texts where the qualifications for local church membership are in addition to membership in the church of Jesus Christ. These have been listed above. No one has shown me textual proof that "formal" local church membership is required for Christians!

I apologize to those offended by my positions listed here, conclusions in Chapter 16 and observations in this chapter. I believe that calling crucified Christians, serving in foreign fields, the parachurch and making a distinction between first-class and covenant, second-class Christians who already belong to the church of the Lord Jesus Christ is, according to the Bible, a gross fallacy, and a blight on contemporary Christianity. I know others may feel differently but this is my story, and I'm comfortable with it.

WHS III

This is my story, this is my song
Praising my Savior all the day long

Perfect submission, all is at rest
I in my Savior am happy and blessed
Watching and waiting, looking above
Filled with His goodness, lost in His love.

This is my story, this is my song
Praising my Savior all the day long.

—*Blessed Assurance, Fanny Crosby*

ABOUT THE FAMILY

I intentionally tried to leave my family out of this book because I had different purposes here. Consequently, there are only a few references to them. However, God has blessed me with a great family. Besides my beautiful wife of almost fifty years, Kathleen, I have five children. Bill Spanjer IV, my oldest son, graduated from our high school (as all of my children did). He went on to earn his Master of Divinity degree from Reformed Theological Seminary (RTS) in Orlando, Florida. He is now pastor of Affirmation Presbyterian Church (PCA). He is now vice president of AEF and director of daily activities at Chapel Field Christian Schools. He and his wife Kristina (also a Chapel Field graduate) have five children.

My second son, Daniel, also graduated from RTS and later earned his doctorate from the University of Albany. He is now serving as chair of the Arts and Sciences Department at Lancaster Bible College. He is married to Tara (a Chapel Field alum), and they have three beautiful girls.

My third son, Timothy Spanjer graduated from Oklahoma Christian College earning a degree in graphic design. He is now the head of marketing at Pursell Farms, a very large corporation in Alabama which supports missionaries around the globe. He is married to Vaughan, and they have three great kids, two girls and one boy.

My fourth son, Stephen Spanjer also graduated from RTS with a Master of Divinity degree and is a missionary and church planter in Germany, where he is the pastor of Neuenburg International Church. He is married to Laura, and they have two wonderful girls.

My last child is Kristen Spanjer. Kristy graduated from Nyack College and later assumed many responsibilities at our Christian school. She also attended RTS where she briefly pursued a master's degree in Christian counseling. She now works for Third Millennium Ministries, a Christian ministry, which develops and freely distributes seminary Bible courses around the globe, primarily to those involved in ministry without the means to attend a brick-and-mortar seminary. She is involved in the curriculum and editing department, which she is able to do from home. Thus she can take care of me.

My mother had one son with my stepfather. His name is Lee Dennett. He and his wonderful wife Jean are serving the Lord full-time in home missions.

On my father's side, he was remarried to a widow, Olga. She is my stepmother and a great lady. She supported me through my high school years and beyond. She had two children. Roger was by her first husband Carl Hansen, who was killed in World War II. Roger married Rachel, and they are leaders in the Methodist church in Perry, Florida. My father and Olga had a daughter, Chrissy. She was a delight to grow up with. Chris was born an artist and now runs an art gallery in Chicago where she lives with her husband, Scott.

Spanjer family, 1984

SOURCES AND REFERENCES

The Amplified Bible, Zondervan Bible Publishers, Grand Rapids, Michigan, 1987

Bainton, Roland H., *Here I Stand: A Life of Martin Luther*, A Mentor Book, 1960

Baker's Dictionary of Theology, Baker Book House, Grand Rapids, Michigan, 1960

Bass, Clarence B., *Backgrounds to Dispensationalism,* William B. Eerdmans Publishing Company, Grand Rapids, Michigan, 1960

Berkhof, L., *Systematic Theology,* Wm B. Eerdmans Publishing Co. Grand Rapids, Michigan, 1941

Bright, John, *The Kingdom of God,* Abingdon Press, Nashville, TN, 1952

Cox, William E., *An Examination of Dispensationalism*, Presbyterian and Reformed Publishing Co., Phillipsburg, New Jersey, 1979

De Rosa, Peter, *Vicars of Christ: The Dark Side of the Papacy,* Crown Publishers, New York, 1988

Emerton, Ephraim, *The Correspondence of Pope Gregory VII: Selected Letters from the Registrum*, Columbia University Press, 1990

Evangelical Dictionary of Theology, Second Ed., Baker Book House Company, Grand Rapids, Michigan, 2001

Hendricksen, William, *The Covenant of Grace,* Wm. B. Eerdmans Publishing Company, 1978

Hendricksen, William, *New Testament Commentary: Exposition of the Gospel According to Matthew,* Baker Book House, Grand Rapids, Michigan, 1973

The Holy Bible: American Standard Version, Thomas Nelson & Sons, New York, NY, 1901

The Holy Bible: Authorized King James Version, Holman Bible Publishers, Nashville, Tennessee,1998

Holy Bible, New International Version, Biblica Inc., 2011

Hymns for the Family of God, Paragon Associates, Inc. Nashville, Tennessee, 1976

New Dictionary of Theology, InterVarsity Press, Downers Grove, Illinois, 1988

Newbigin, Leslie, *The Household of God,* Friendship Press, Inc., New York, 1954

Ramm, Bernard, *Protestant Biblical Interpretation: A Textbook of Hermeneutics for Conservative Protestants,* W. A. Wilde Company, Boston, 1956

Renwick, A.M. & Harmon, A.M., *The Story of the Church,* Second and Enlarged Edition, William B. Eerdmans Publishing Company, Grand Rapids, Michigan, 1985

Riddlebarger, Kim, *A Case for Amillennialism: Understanding the End Times,* Baker Book House, Grand Rapids, Michigan, 2003

Roberts, Frank C., *To All Generations: A Study of Church History,* Bible Way, Grand Rapids, Michigan, 1981

Sproul, R.C., *What is Reformed Theology,* Ligonier Ministries, 1997

Spurgeon, C. H., *An All-Round Ministry: Addresses to Ministers and Students,* The Banner of Truth Trust, Carlisle, Pennsylvania, 1986

Vine, W. E., *An Expository Dictionary of New Testament Words: with their Precise Meanings for English Readers,* Fleming H. Revell Company, Westwood, New Jersey, 1966